# THE COMPLETE BOOK OF
# home
# stenciling

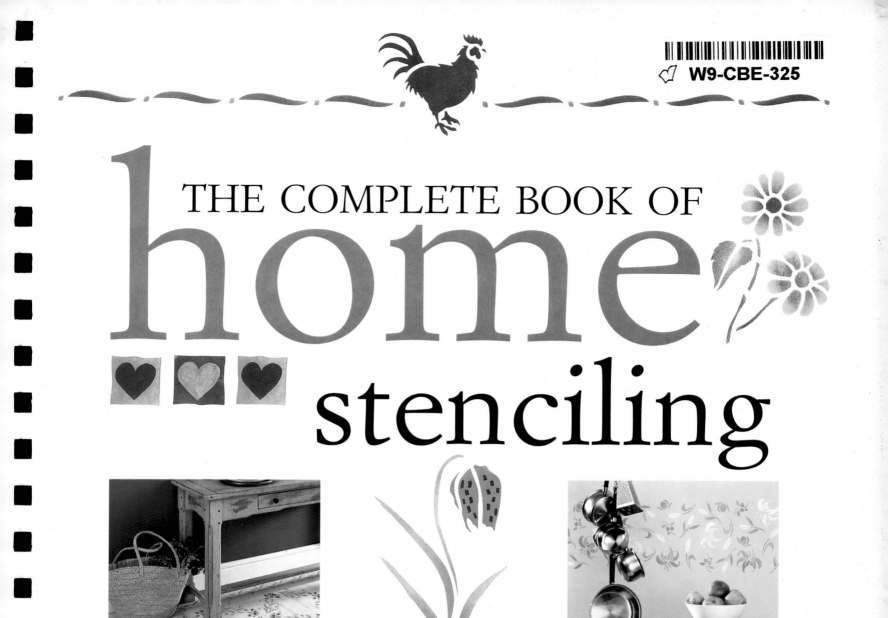

Katrina Hall

Denise Westcott
Taylor

MURDOCH
B O O K S

# Contents

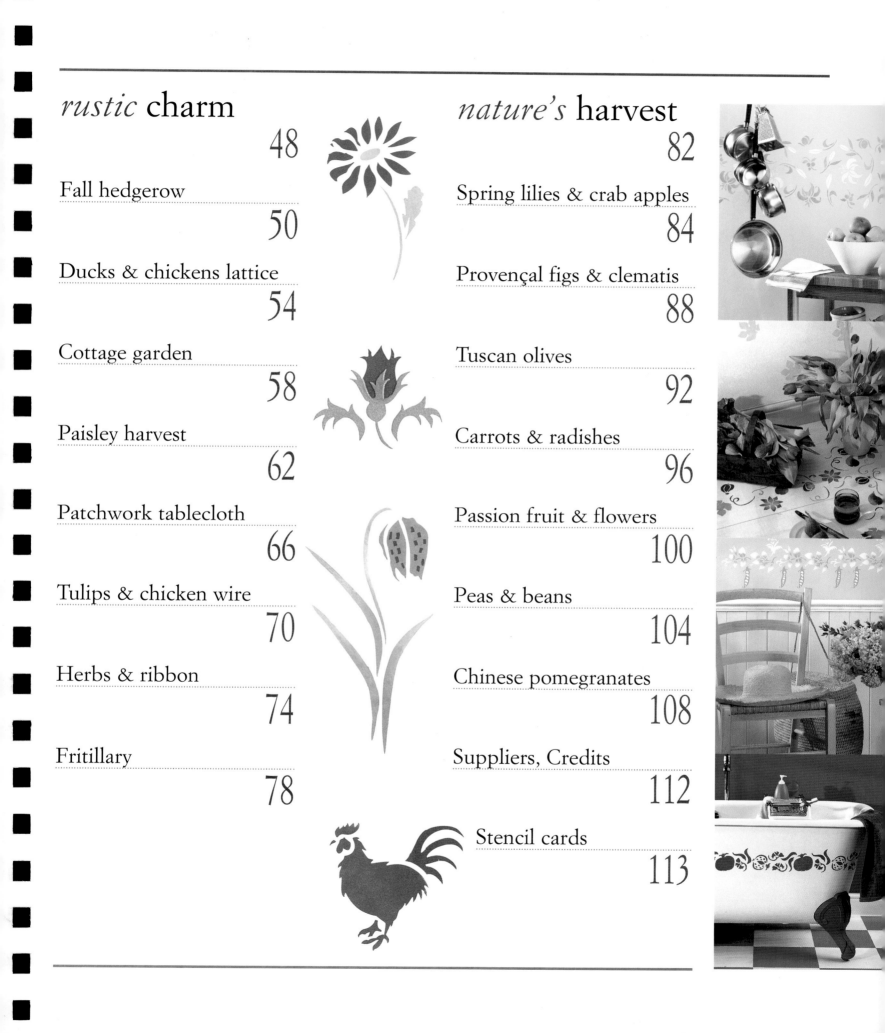

# INTRODUCING STENCILING

Once you begin stenciling you will be amazed at the wonderful results you can obtain easily and without spending a great deal of money. This book introduces six themed projects and provides ready-to-use stencils that can be used with numerous variations in design—just follow the step-by-step features and simple instructions. With very little paint and only a few pieces of equipment, you can achieve stunning results. Have fun!

## BASIC MATERIALS

### Paints and Decorative Finishes
Latex paint
Water-based stencil paint
Oil sticks
Acrylic paints (bottles and tubes)
Specialized paints (for fabrics, ceramics, etc)
Spray paints
Metallic acrylic artist's colors (gold, silver, etc)
Silver and gold art flow pens
Bronze powders (various metallics)
Gilt wax

### Brushes and Applicators
Art brushes (variety of sizes)
Stencil brushes (small, medium, and large)
Sponge applicators
Miniroller and tray

### Other Equipment
Carpenter's square
Blotting paper
Scissors or craft knife
Roll of craft paper (for practicing)
Eraser
Soft pencil
Fine-tipped permanent marker pen
Chalk, or chalkline and powdered chalk
Long rigid ruler
Tape measure
Plumb line
Carpenter's level
Low-tack masking tape
Spray adhesive
Tracing paper
Paint dishes or palettes
Cloths
Paper towels
Mineral spirits
Stencil plastic or card stock
Cotton swabs
Denatured alcohol

**CUTTING OUT STENCILS**
The stencils at the back of the book are designed to be used separately or together to create many different pattern combinations. Cut along the dotted lines of the stencils and make sure you transfer the reference code onto each one with a permanent pen. Carefully remove the cutout pieces of the stencil. Apply 2" (50 mm) strips of tracing paper around the edges using masking tape; this will help to keep paint from smudging onto your surface.

**REPAIRING STENCILS**
Stencils may become damaged and torn from mishandling, or if the cutouts have not been removed carefully, but they are easy to repair. Keeping the stencil perfectly flat, cover both sides of the tear with masking tape. Carefully remove any excess tape with a craft knife.

# GETTING STARTED

### DUPLICATING STENCILS
Use stencil plastic (Mylar) or card stock wiped with linseed oil, which will harden when dry and make the surface waterproof. Place the cutout stencil on top. Carefully trace around the cutout shapes with a permanent pen. Cut along the lines with a craft knife and remove the pieces. You may prefer to trace the stencil design first, then transfer your tracing onto stencil plastic or card stock.

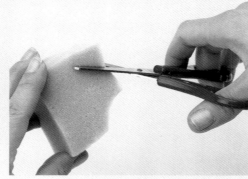

### MAKING A SPONGE APPLICATOR
Sponging your stencil is one of the easiest methods (however, you may prefer to use a stencil brush, especially for fine detail). To make a sponge applicator, cut ½–2" (12–50 mm) wide and 2" (50 mm) long pieces of upholstery foam or dense bath sponge. Hold four of the corners together and secure with tape to form a pad. You can also round off the ends with scissors or a craft knife and trim to a smooth finish. Use the small-ended applicators for tiny, intricate patterns.

### HOW TO USE WATER-BASED PAINT
Water-based paints are easy and economical to use, and have the advantage of drying quickly. For professional-looking stencils, do not load your sponge or brush too heavily or you will not achieve a soft, shaded finish. Paint that is too watery will seep under the stencil edges and smudge. Paint that is too heavy will produce a dense, block effect rather than the soft stippling you require.

### LOOKING AFTER STENCILS
Stencils have a long life if cared for correctly. Before cleaning, make sure you remove any tape or tracing paper that has been added. Remove any excess paint before it dries, and wipe the stencil with a damp cloth after each use. If water-based or acrylic paint has dried and hardened, soften it with water and ease it off gently with a craft knife. Then use a small amount of denatured alcohol on a cloth to remove the rest. An oil-based paint can be removed simply by wiping the stencil with mineral spirits on a cloth. Stencils should be dried thoroughly before storing flat between sheets of waxed paper.

### HOW TO USE OIL STICKS
Oil sticks may seem expensive, but in fact go a long way. They take longer to dry than water-based paints, allowing you to blend colors very effectively. Oil-stick paint should be applied with a stencil brush, and you will need a different brush for each color. Break the seal as instructed on the stick and rub a patch of the color onto a palette, allowing space to blend colors. As oil-stick paint dries slowly, you need to lift the stencil off cleanly, and then replace to continue the pattern.

### PRACTICING PAINTING STENCILS
Roll out some craft paper onto a table and select the stencil you wish to practice. Using spray adhesive, lightly spray the back of your stencil and place it into position on the paper. Prepare your paint on a palette. Dab your sponge or brush into the paint and offload excess paint onto scrap paper. Apply color over the stencil in a light coat to create an even, stippled effect. You can always stencil on a little more paint if a stronger effect is needed, but if you overapply it in the first place, it is very difficult to remove. Keep separate sponges for different colors.

# PLANNING YOUR DESIGN

Before starting to stencil, take time to plan your design. Decide where you want to use the patterns, then figure out how to position the stencils so that the design will fit around obstacles such as doorways and corners. The techniques shown here will help you to undertake the job with a systematic approach.

### PUTTING PATTERN PIECES TOGETHER

1 Before you apply your design, stencil a sample onto craft paper. Mark the center and baseline of the design on the paper and put together your pattern pieces. You can then figure out the size of the design, how it will fit into the space available, and the distance required between repeats.

2 You can avoid stenciling around a corner by calculating the number of pattern repeats needed, and then increasing the space between repeats or within the pattern accordingly. Creating vertical lines through the pattern will allow you to stretch it evenly.

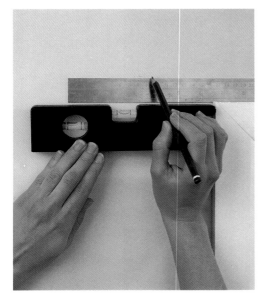

### MARKING BASELINES AND HORIZONTAL LINES

Select your stencil area, and measure from the ceiling, doorframe, window, or edging, bearing in mind the depth of your stencil. Using a level, mark a horizontal line. You can then extend this by using a chalkline, or a long ruler with chalk or a soft pencil.

### MARKING VERTICAL LINES

If you need to calculate the vertical position for a stencil, hang a plumb line above the stenciling area and use a ruler to draw a vertical line with chalk or a soft pencil. You will need to use this method when creating an all-over wallpaper design.

### FIXING THE STENCIL INTO PLACE

Lightly spray the back of the stencil with spray adhesive, then put it in position and smooth it down carefully. You can use low-tack masking tape if you prefer, but take care not to damage the surface to be stenciled. The stencil should be flat to keep paint from seeping underneath.

### MARKING THE STENCIL FOR A PATTERN REPEAT

Attach tracing paper to each edge of the stencil. Position the next pattern, overlapping the tracing paper onto the previous design and tracing around the edge of it. As you work along a surface, match the tracing with the previous pattern to help you align and repeat the stencil at regular intervals.

### COPING WITH CORNERS

Stencil around corners after you have finished the rest of the design, having measured to leave the correct space for the corner pattern before you do so. Bend the stencil into the corner and mask off one side of it. Stencil the open side and allow the paint to dry, then mask off this half and stencil the remaining part to complete the design.

### MASKING OFF PART OF A STENCIL

Use low-tack masking tape to mask out small or intricate areas of stencil. You can use ordinary masking tape, but remove excess stickiness first by peeling it on and off your skin or a cloth once or twice. To block off inside shapes and large areas, cut out pieces of tracing paper to the appropriate size and fix them on top with spray adhesive.

### MITERING STENCIL PATTERNS

1 When you are stenciling a continuous pattern and need to make a corner, mark a 45-degree angle at both ends of the stencil with a permanent pen. Mask along this line with a piece of masking tape or tracing paper.

2 Make sure the baselines of the stencil on both sides of the corner are the same distance from the edge, and that they cross at the corner. Put the diagonal end of the stencil right into the corner and apply the paint. Turn the stencil sidewise to align the other diagonal end of the stencil and turn the corner.

# PAINT EFFECTS

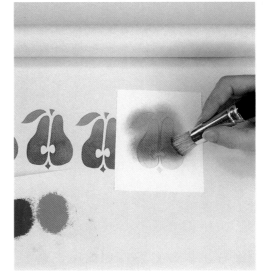

### CHOOSING COLORS

Take care to choose appropriate colors to create the effect you want. Practice the stencil design on paper, and try a variation of colors to make sure you are pleased with the result. Different colors can make a design look entirely different. Use spray adhesive to fix your practice paper onto the surface on which you wish to produce the design so that you can assess its effect before applying the stencil.

### APPLYING WATER-BASED COLORS

Water-based paint dries quickly, so it tends to layer rather than blend. It is best to apply it using a swirling movement or gentle dabbing, depending on the finished effect you wish to create. Once you have applied a light base color, you can add a darker edge for shading. Or leave some of the stencil bare and add a different tone in that area to obtain a shaded or highlighted appearance.

### BLENDING OIL-STICK COLORS

Oil-stick paints mix together smoothly so they are perfect for blending colors. Place the colors separately on your palette and mix them with white to obtain a variety of tones, or blend them together to create new colors. You can also blend by applying one coat into another with a stippling motion while stenciling. Blending looks most effective when applying a pale base coat, then shading on top with a darker color.

### HIGHLIGHTING

A simple way to add highlighting to a design is first to paint your stencil in a light tone of the main color, then carefully lift the stencil and move it down a fraction. Now stencil in a darker shade; this leaves the highlighted areas around the top edges of the pattern.

### GILDING

After painting your stencil, use gold to highlight the edges. Load a fine art brush with gold acrylic paint and carefully outline the top edges of the pattern. Use one quick brush stroke for each pattern repeat, always working in the same direction. Other gilding methods include blowing bronze powder onto the wet paint, drawing around the pattern with a gold art flow pen, or smudging on gilt wax cream and then buffing to a high sheen.

### APPLYING SPRAY PAINTS

Spray paints are ideal on glass, wood, metal, plastic, and ceramic surfaces. They are quick to apply and fast drying, but they cannot be blended, although you can achieve subtle shaded effects. Apply the paint in several thin coats, masking off a large area around the design to protect it from the spray, which tends to drift. Use sprays outdoors or in a well-ventilated area. Some spray paints are nontoxic, making them ideal for children's furniture.

# DIFFERENT SURFACES

### RAW WOOD

Rub down the wood surface to a smooth finish. Fix the stencil in place and apply a thin base coat of white, so that the stencil colors will stand out well when applied. Leave the stencil in place and let the paint dry thoroughly, then apply your stencil colors in the normal way. When completely dry, you can apply a coat of light wax or varnish to protect your stencil.

### PAINTED WOOD

If you are painting wood or manufactured wood products (MDF) prior to stenciling, seal it with a coat of acrylic primer before adding a base coat of latex or acrylic paint. If the base coat is dark, stencil a thin coat of white paint on top. Apply your stencil, and if required, protect with a coat of clear varnish when it is completely dry.

### FABRIC

Use special fabric paint for stenciling on fabric, and follow the manufacturer's instructions carefully. Place card or blotting paper behind the fabric while working, and keep the material taut. If you are painting a dark fabric, best results are achieved by stenciling first with white or a light shade. Heat seal the design following the manufacturer's instructions.

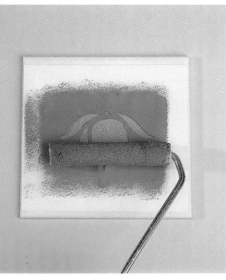

### CERAMICS

Use special ceramic paints to work directly onto glazed ceramic tiles and unglazed ceramics such as terra cotta. Make sure all surfaces are clean, so that the stencils can be fixed easily. Apply the paint with a brush, sponge, spray, or miniroller. Ceramic paints are durable and washable, and full manufacturer's instructions are given on the container.

### GLASS

Before applying the stencil, make sure the glass is clean, then spray on a light coat of adhesive and position the stencil. Spray on water-based or ceramic paint, remove the stencil, and allow to dry. If you wish to stencil drinking glasses, use special nontoxic and water-resistant glass paints. You can achieve an etched-glass look with stencils on windows, doors, and mirrors with a variety of materials.

### PAINTED SURFACES

Stencils can be applied to surfaces painted with flat or satin latex emulsion, oil-based scumble glazes, acrylic glazes, and varnishes, as well as to matte wallpaper. If you wish to decorate a gloss surface, stencil first with an acrylic primer, let it dry, and then stencil the colors on top. Surfaces to be stenciled need to be smooth so that the stencil can lie flat.

# *flower* power

Flowers have always been a source of inspiration for artists and interior designers. Their varied forms and colors provide an endless palette of ideas for stenciling. This chapter shows a range of different flower stencils, from the humble dandelion to the noble rose, and from the simple daisy to the delicate forget-me-not. Each project shows how both the flower itself and its foliage work together, making a wonderful pattern to suit different rooms and styles in your home.

# DANDELIONS

Most gardeners have a love/hate relationship with the dandelion—this flower grows and spreads like wildfire, plaguing lawns with long roots that are very difficult to dig up. To children, however, dandelions are heaven-sent to "tell the time" by blowing the feathery seed heads on summer afternoons. A mesh cupboard is an ideal piece for this project, giving it a "potting shed" feel. The leaves and flowers are joined to create dandelion plants growing from the bottom of the cupboard, with seeds floating above and a snail sneaking in.

## PAINT COLOR GUIDE

White spray paint

### DECORATING THE CUPBOARD DOORS

**1** Paint the cupboard's wood sections with an all-in-one primer/undercoat in white. Paint a couple of layers of white latex on top. You may be able to use just one layer, depending how thick the paint is.

**2** Make a wash by diluting stone-colored latex paint with water. Put the color on and carefully drag it off with a dry brush to give an "old" wood effect. Work the paint in the direction of the wood sections of the cupboard, emphasizing the joints. When dry, give the wood a few coats of varnish.

**3** The door knobs are stones with holes through the middle, tied on with string.

**4** Paint the dandelion stencils on the mesh using white spray paint. Practice on a spare piece of mesh. If you make a mistake, mix some silver and black paint to neaten the edges.

### PROJECT PATTERN

The dandelion plants are built up by combining the different leaves and stalks (used in reverse and upside down), topped with flowers and seed heads (dandelion clocks). The seeds are in the same pattern on each side, although the overall look is random.

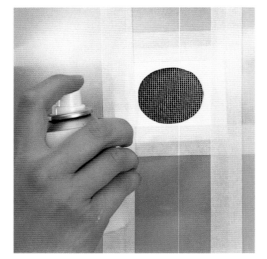

**SPRAYING THE BASE COLOR**
Make sure that the stencils are fixed securely with spray adhesive, then spray the paint in thin layers to give a well-defined edge. Spray the background of the seed head (stencil D) lightly to give the faint impression of a globe, before painting the individual seeds (stencil A) on top.

**BUILDING UP LAYERS**
To achieve a more opaque finish, spray lightly, building up thin layers. Make sure that each element is dry before you move onto the next. Be careful not to overspray, as the mesh holes can clog up easily.

**CREATING THE SNAIL STENCIL**
Create a trail of snails (stencil E) around a pot, along the front of shelves, or on top of baseboards. A simple element in a single color can be low-key or dramatic, depending on the color you use and how densely you apply it.

# DANDELIONS VARIATIONS

This project provides endless opportunities for creative decoration. You can use greens and yellows to form realistic-looking dandelion plants, or choose the individual elements to build up many other designs, as shown here in greens, turquoises, and blues. Do not be afraid to experiment with the different shapes as pure pattern, rather than restricting yourself to the realistic growth pattern of the actual plant.

**STAR EDGING (STENCIL A)**

**LEAF CIRCLE (STENCIL J)**

**SNAIL TRAIL (STENCIL E)**

**LEAF BORDER (STENCIL J)**

**SEED HEAD DESIGN (STENCILS A, D, F, AND H)**

**LEAF WHEEL (STENCIL G)**

**SNOWFLAKE MOTIF (STENCIL B)**

**NARROW LEAF DIAMOND BORDER (STENCIL G)**

**STAR MEDALLION (STENCIL A)**

**SEED HEAD DESIGN (STENCILS A, D, F, AND H)**

**FLOWER CORNER (STENCIL C)**

**REGIMENTAL SEEDS ROW (STENCIL B)**

**ABOVE: LEAF BORDER (STENCIL J)**

**FLOWER AND STALK REPEAT (STENCILS C AND I)**

**SEED SQUARE REPEAT (STENCIL B)**

## PAINT COLOR GUIDE

White       Yellow       Red

Green

### STENCILING ONTO FABRIC

1 Wash the fabric before painting to remove any finishes. Press well.

2 When stenciling onto fabric, use as dry a brush as possible to keep paint from seeping under the stencil. Fabric paints are available in a limited number of colors, so mix the yellow and red paints for additional warm yellows and oranges.

3 Position the stems (stencils B and D) before placing the flowers and leaves.

4 Fix fabric paint according to the manufacturer's instructions.

# SUNSHINE DAISIES

T his sunny daisy design seems to conjure up all the warmth of summer. Stenciled onto table linen, these flowers will brighten any meal and bring glowing compliments from guests. Placemats could be stenciled to match the tablecloth. Stenciling onto fabric requires confidence because mistakes cannot be wiped away, but with a little practice, this project is well within the reach of a beginner.

The table linen here has been painted in warm yellows, but the flowers would look equally striking in other bright colors.

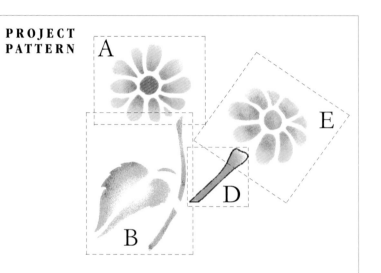

**PROJECT PATTERN**

A   E   D   B

### POSITIONING THE STENCIL
Use parts of the stem (stencil B) and flower stencils to make a bunch, masking areas not to be painted. Hold the stencil firmly in place on the fabric with spray adhesive. Reposition the stencils carefully for each subsequent color you apply.

### PAINTING THE STENCIL
When working on a colored fabric, paint the whole design in white before applying the colors. Allow the white paint to dry and fix according to the manufacturer's instructions before adding the colors. This gives a good background for the subsequent colors.

### ADDING THE COLORS
Use a clean sponge to apply pale yellow for the petals. Let the yellow paint dry and fix it before adding more colors. Paint a rich orange-red in the center for the stamens. Overlap the colors to produce a gradual change.

# SUNSHINE DAISIES VARIATIONS

The Sunshine Daisies stencils look good on walls and furniture as well as on fabric. Paint a border of flower heads in the breakfast room to complement your tablecloth. The circle of leaves is formed by overlapping a leaf stencil, taking care not to paint over the previous leaf. Try painting the flowers in different colors and flipping the stencils to create a posy.

**LEAF CIRCLE (STENCIL C)**

**DAISIES (STENCILS A, B, AND E)**

**BUNCH OF DAISIES
(STENCILS A AND E)**

**DAISY
EDGING
(STENCIL D)**

**DAISY AND LEAF
BORDER (STENCILS
A AND B)**

**LEAF BORDER (STENCIL C)**

CLIMBING LEAVES FRAME (STENCIL B)

TWO DAISIES BORDER
(STENCILS A, B, AND E)

DAISY BORDER
(STENCIL E)

DAISY CHAIN
(STENCILS B AND E)

## PAINT COLOR GUIDE

Cobalt blue    Deep purple

Lime green    White

### DECORATING WOODEN BOXES

**1** Coat the raw wood with all-in-one primer/undercoat, then top it with a thin layer of baby blue. You may need to apply a couple of coats, with a sanding session in between, to produce a smooth surface.

**2** If you make a mistake on the box, it is difficult to fix, so practice the design on paper first to make sure all the elements fit. When you are ready, stencil your design.

**3** Stenciled surfaces benefit from at least two layers of varnish for protection. Water-based varnish is usually sufficient, but use oil-based varnish for a surface that will receive heavy use or that needs to be heat resistant.

# FORGET-ME-NOTS

**F**orget-me-nots twist and twine their way among all the other wildflowers of the hedgerows and woodlands. These delicate-looking flowers seem to grow wild where gardens end and bluebell woods begin—that magical place where fairies dance. Combine blues, purples, and greens with white flower centers to keep the project looking clean and fresh. Even though the boxes are decorated differently, a continuous row around the tops of the boxes links the design together.

### PROJECT PATTERN

The border on both boxes is a simple repeat of stencil C. For the small box pattern, rotate stencil D. The design on the large box is achieved by combining small sections of stencils with whole stencils.

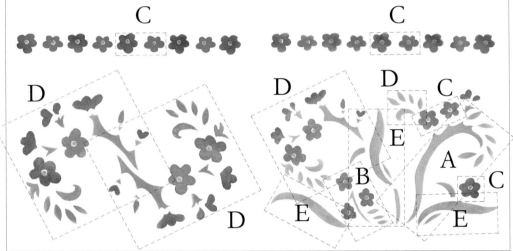

**DOUBLE-LAYERING THE PAINT**
To achieve the effect of double-layered paint, apply the first coat and let it dry thoroughly. Reposition the stencil, then apply the second color with a very dry brush, using big, swirling strokes.

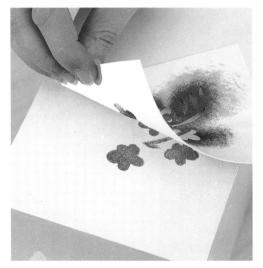

**CHECKING THE COLORS**
Turn back the edge of a stencil to preview the colors and check the effect. You may want to add color or depth in places, and it is easier to do so while the stencil is still in position.

**PLACING THE FLOWER CENTERS**
Use a cotton swab to add the flower centers. The best way is to paint a piece of paper in white, and then use the paper as a paint reservoir to regulate your paint quantity. It is surprising how little paint you need.

# FORGET-ME-NOTS VARIATIONS

T he natural colors of these flowers range from light blues to mauves and pinks, giving you a great deal of room to experiment. Try adding turquoise and yellow to blues and lime greens. Do not feel restricted by the smallness of the Forget-Me-Nots pattern. It could easily be transformed into a wide border, or applied to the panels of a door or around a hat box.

**STALK AND LEAF OVALS (STENCIL E)**

**ENTWINED STALKS (STENCIL A)**

**LEAF CORNER (STENCIL E)**

**CURLING STALKS (STENCIL E)**

**FORGET-ME-NOT MOTIF (STENCIL D)**

**CURLING SPRIGS (STENCIL B)**

LINKING TENDRILS MOTIF (STENCIL A)

FORGET-ME-NOT BORDER (STENCIL B)

CURLING SPRIGS STRIPE
(STENCIL B)

TENDRILS
RIBBON
(STENCIL A)

FORGET-ME-NOT SWAGS (STENCIL D)

CHAIN OF FLOWERS
(STENCIL C)

# MORNING GLORY

The beautiful climbing plant Morning Glory will bring the freshness of the garden into your home, and is ideal for brightening a bedroom. Here, the stencil has been painted to resemble striped wallpaper, but has the appeal of hand-painted decoration. Stripes of climbing leaves alternate with ropes twisted about with flowers.

The blooms and buds are added singly and appear to "grow" from the stems. Other items could be decorated with some of the smaller stencils for a coordinated look.

## PAINT COLOR GUIDE

| | | |
|---|---|---|
| Pale gray | Gray-green | Lavender |
| Mauve | Light blue | |

### POSITIONING AND PAINTING

1 Use a plumb line to mark the vertical positions of the "stripes." Measure and space the stencils accurately.

2 The stem (stencil F) fits between the segments of the rope (stencil A). Practice the design on paper, painting the rope first and then the stem. Only part of the stem needs to be painted. Do not paint over the rope, so that the stem appears to twist around the rope.

3 Paint flowers and leaves (stencils C and E) so that they appear to grow naturally.

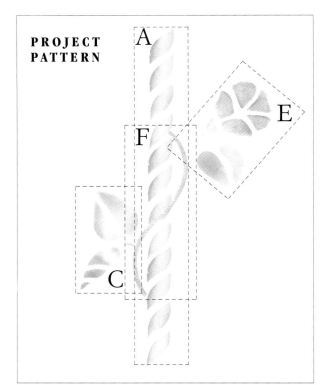

PROJECT PATTERN

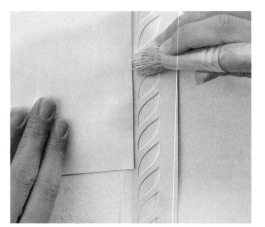

### ENHANCING THE ROPE
To make the rope look more realistic, paint it darker on the side that is farthest from the window and lighter on the other side, giving a three-dimensional appearance.

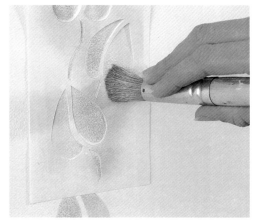

### PAINTING THE LEAVES
Use a brush to paint the leaves in gray-green and pale gray, blending the colors for a two-tone effect. Make areas of the leaves lighter or darker to suggest highlights and shadows. Brush on the color using a circular action for a soft effect.

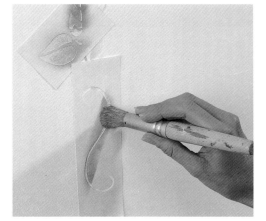

### ADDING THE FLOWERS
Position the stem (stencil F) so that it fits between two segments of the rope (stencil A). Paint it carefully, masking the area covering the rope. Add flowers to the stems, changing their positions and reversing some of them for a realistic effect.

# MORNING GLORY VARIATIONS

The flowers and leaves of the Morning Glory stencils can be used singly or combined in borders and motifs, and this design is particularly suited to trailing effects. The stem stencil can also be used on its own to make some very smart designs reminiscent of wrought ironwork. Miter the ends of the rope to make a frame and paint some flowers in the center.

**LEAF AND FLOWER (STENCIL E)**

**ROPE EDGING (STENCIL A)**

**DOUBLE SCROLL BORDER (STENCIL F)**

**LEAVES BORDER (STENCIL B)**

**FLOWER AND BUD BORDER (STENCIL D)**

ROPE EDGING (STENCIL A)

BUD AND LEAF PATTERN
(STENCIL C)

FLOWER AND BUD SPRAY
(STENCIL D)

TRAILING LEAVES BORDER (STENCIL B)

SCROLL EDGING (STENCIL F)

LEAF AND BUD BORDER (STENCIL C)

FLOWER, BUD, AND SCROLL BORDER (STENCILS C, E, AND F)

# POPPIES

Poppies conjure up the quintessential hazy feeling of a midsummer's day. In this project the combination of yellow ocher, deep purple, red, and fiery orange creates a harmonious warm atmosphere. Spiky leaves, curvaceous poppy flowers with dark seductive centers, rounded seed heads, gently bending buds, and bumble bees fuse to form a sympathetic union of shapes. Together the colors and shapes convey the feeling of walking through a field of golden grain, dotted with the richness of red and orange wildflowers.

## PAINT COLOR GUIDE

Deep purple    Dark red    Fiery orange

### PAINTING THE FRAME

1 Paint the frame with all-in-one primer/undercoat and then apply two layers of yellow ocher latex paint.

2 Mix a wash with the consistency of light cream, using a burnt umber acrylic and latex glaze. Gently apply the wash with big brushstrokes, working across the frame so that there is a hint of color.

3 Apply the large poppy (stencils E, G, and F) in the corners of the frame and add the other elements in a random pattern. Finish the frame by painting the inner and outer edges with a rich red to give the sides definition.

### PROJECT PATTERN

In this random design, the most difficult element is the poppy flower. Place stencil E first and then put stencil G carefully on top. Finish with stencil F, to complete the flower.

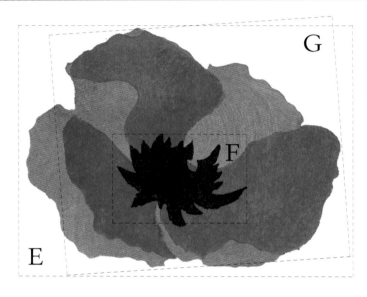

### POSITIONING WITH CUTOUTS

To position the stencils, make paper cutouts and move the shapes around until you are happy with the design. Start with the larger shapes and fill in the gaps with the smaller ones. Let some shapes overlap the frame.

### CHECKING WITH TRACING PAPER

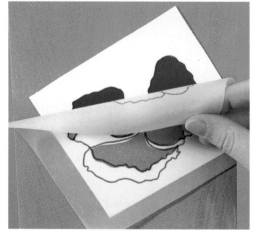

To create the large poppy petals, apply stencil G over stencil E. Position the two parts by using tracing paper to make a drawing of the way the shapes fit together. After stenciling the bottom shape (stencil E), slide the top shape (stencil G) under the tracing paper, then remove the paper.

### KEEPING COLORS CLEAN

When using two colors within the same shape, work from opposite ends of the stencil with each one. Combine the colors in the middle with a different brush to keep the tones clean and clear.

# POPPIES VARIATIONS

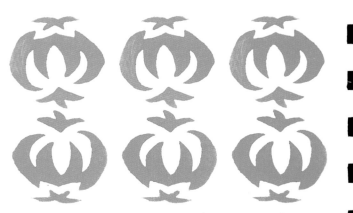

B y adding pinks and yellow ocher to your palette of rich reds, oranges, and purples, you can move the design of this project toward the Orient to give a more mysterious feel, or to India for a more exotic look. If you are adventurous, you could make realistic poppy plants look as if they are growing out of the baseboards, or create entire poppy fields on the walls.

**SEED HEAD EDGING (STENCIL C)**

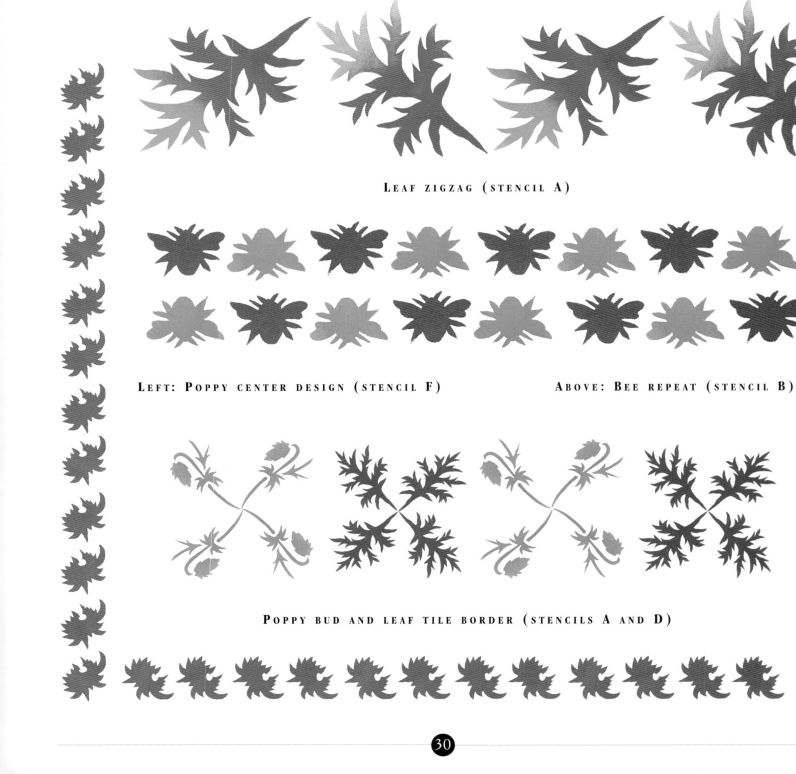

**LEAF ZIGZAG (STENCIL A)**

**LEFT: POPPY CENTER DESIGN (STENCIL F)**

**ABOVE: BEE REPEAT (STENCIL B)**

**POPPY BUD AND LEAF TILE BORDER (STENCILS A AND D)**

**POPPY HEAD REPEAT (STENCILS E, F, AND G)**

**BUZZING BEES (STENCIL B)**

**LEAF TILE (STENCIL A)**

**POPPY BUD TILE
(STENCIL D)**

**LINKED POPPY BUD BORDER (STENCIL D)**

**SEED HEAD
STRIPE
(STENCIL C)**

**POPPY BUD
BORDER
(STENCIL D)**

# DAISIES & WILD ROSEBUDS

**W**hile daisies may threaten the image of a perfect green lawn, daisy chains are an important part of childhood, forming the basis for imaginative bracelets, necklaces, and crowns. Later on, plucked single petals provide answers to whether someone "loves me, loves me not." Wild hedge roses do not lend themselves so readily to games, but their thorny wildness has a charm of its own. This stencil design combines the rigid qualities of the daisy and the rambling habit of the wild rose.

## PAINT COLOR GUIDE

Lime green    Brilliant white

Pinkish red    Bright yellow

### PAINTING THE HEADBOARD

**1** Sand the whole headboard well before you start—nothing could be worse than leaning on sharp wooden edges.

**2** Apply a couple of layers of latex paint to the headboard to cover up any existing paintwork. Once the paintwork has dried, apply a light-green glaze.

**3** It is worth testing the glaze with the stencil colors on top. In this project you are working with shades of paints that are lighter or darker than the background and you may want to alter the balance. Apply the stencils when you are happy with the effect.

### PROJECT PATTERN

Once you have stenciled the outside squares, the center is simply a daisy or rosebud. To achieve the rose, start with the bud (stencil E) and work the sepals (stencil B) on top.

### POSITIONING THE GINGHAM PATTERN

Plot the position of the pattern of squares by marking a grid faintly in pencil. You can erase these lines when you have finished stenciling, but make sure the paint is totally dry before you do so.

### PROTECTING THE EDGES

Mask the edges of the headboard panels to protect the glazed woodwork from the stencil colors. Patching up smudged paintwork is virtually impossible unless you have applied a couple of layers of acrylic varnish, when you can usually wash off the smudge with a wet cloth.

### ADDING PINK TIPS TO THE PETALS

To emphasize and enliven the daisy petal edges, add a deep pink to the tips. Do this when the white paint is totally dry, so that the ends are blushed with color.

# DAISIES & WILD ROSEBUDS
# VARIATIONS

These rosebuds lend themselves to a retro 1950s wallpaper style. Put the stencils on a robin's egg blue, mint-green, or pale-yellow background, and use pinks and reds for the rosebuds themselves. Link daisies into chains to create a linear pattern that could adorn any number of items. Stencils F and H can be combined into gingham stripes by slipping one over the other.

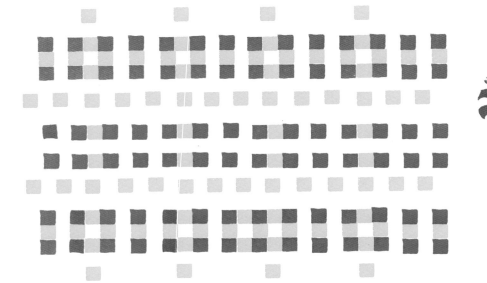

**DOUBLE STRIPE (STENCIL H) WITH SINGLE STRIPE (STENCIL F)**

**ALL-OVER DAISY CHAIN DESIGN (STENCILS A AND G)**

**DAISY CORNER (STENCIL A)**

**LEAF CIRCLES (STENCIL C)**

**LEAF BORDER CORNER (STENCILS C AND D)**

**LINE OF BUDS (STENCIL E)**

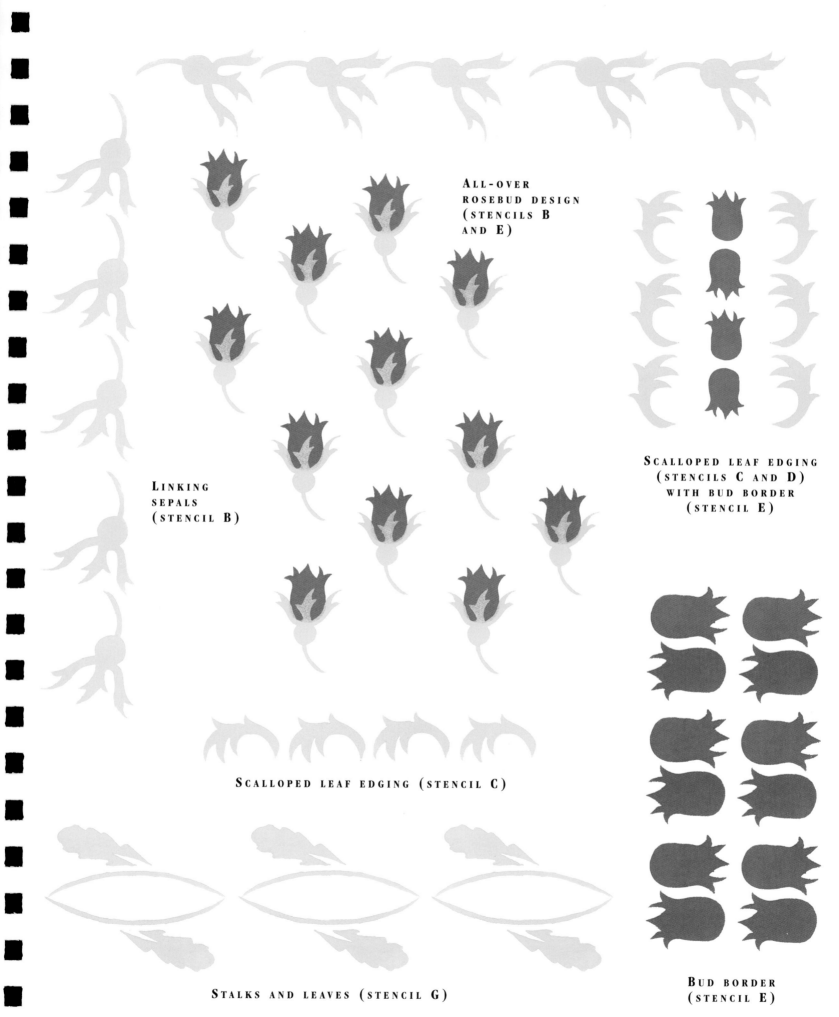

**ALL-OVER ROSEBUD DESIGN (STENCILS B AND E)**

**LINKING SEPALS (STENCIL B)**

**SCALLOPED LEAF EDGING (STENCILS C AND D) WITH BUD BORDER (STENCIL E)**

**SCALLOPED LEAF EDGING (STENCIL C)**

**STALKS AND LEAVES (STENCIL G)**

**BUD BORDER (STENCIL E)**

## PAINT COLOR GUIDE

Light blue    Deep blue

Forest green    Pine green

### PAINTING THE FLOORBOARDS

1 Raw wooden floors need to be well sanded before you can start painting. Start with a coarse-grit sandpaper and gradually move onto finer grits once the really rough patches have been dealt with.

2 Apply a wood wash. Either buy a readymade one or dilute white latex paint with water; it is a matter of trial and error to mix the density you require.

3 The wash dries very quickly, so work with a single plank at a time to avoid join marks.

4 Follow the project pattern to apply the stencil design. Protect the floor afterwards with an oil-based wood varnish.

# CORNFLOWERS & BUTTERFLIES

Cornflowers—bright-blue thistlelike flowers with jagged petals, spindly stalks, and long leaves—are visited by gentle butterflies in the design for this floor project. By painting the different elements in clean blues and greens on whitewashed wooden boards, the feeling is of Scandinavian style. The large repeat allows the pattern to have an organic look, with leaves twisting and turning and the flowers stretching up to the sun. Butterflies hover and occasionally land to rest on a leaf.

### PROJECT PATTERN

The pattern is built up using stencils A, C, D, E, and F. Part of stencil E is repeated to provide a curly leaf to balance the design. The flanking leaf border is simply a repeat of stencil F.

---

**TRACING THE PATTERN REPEAT**
Having planned your pattern repeat, it can be useful to do a tracing of the entire repeat. Lift it up and down to check that all the elements of the design are in position and fit into the space you are tackling.

**ADDING FORM TO THE LEAVES**
To make your design look three-dimensional rather than flat, paint the leaves more realistically by adding a darker shade to the twists and underneath sections, which gives them a more rounded quality.

**ADDING DETAIL WITH A BRUSH**
Adding more detail by hand can improve a design enormously. In this project, only the butterflies received this treatment. This technique can be useful to create a more hand-painted and individual look than that produced by using a repeated pattern.

# CORNFLOWERS & BUTTERFLIES VARIATIONS

By simply curving the existing pattern repeat used in the floor project, and adding a few leaves and butterflies, you could create swags of spring flowers. Or just use single elements for a much simpler design, perhaps repeating a motif to establish an uncomplicated border. These stencil designs are very adaptable. A deep purple for the cornflower blooms goes well with sage-green leaves and stems.

**CORNFLOWER ROW (STENCILS A AND F)**

**LITTLE BUTTERFLIES (STENCIL D)**

**CURLING LEAVES STRIPE (STENCIL E)**

**CORNFLOWER FRIEZE (STENCIL A)**

**CURLING LEAVES BORDER (STENCIL E)**

**SWAG (STENCILS A, C, D, E, AND F)**

**LINKING BUDS (STENCIL C)**

**BUTTERFLY STRIPES (STENCIL B)**

**LEAF LATTICE TILE (STENCIL F)**

**CURLING LEAVES BORDER (STENCIL E)**
**WITH LITTLE BUTTERFLIES (STENCIL D)**

**SIMPLE BUD REPEAT**
**(STENCIL C)**

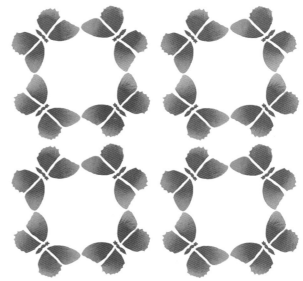

**TWISTING LEAVES (STENCIL F)**

**BUTTERFLY TILES (STENCIL B)**

# INDIAN BLOOMS

Re-create the heat and mystery of the East with these Indian blooms. Flower and leaf designs are used extensively in Indian textiles; these stencils were inspired by fabrics from northern India. Traditionally, such materials are produced in rich colors, so this room has been stenciled with reds, pink, and green with gold highlights to create a warm, exotic design. The simplicity of the designs makes them versatile, and the trailing ribbon is particularly suitable to use with other stencils in this book.

## PAINT COLOR GUIDE

Cream     Terra cotta     Crimson red

Rust red     Rose red     Apple green

Gold (artist's acrylic)

### COLOR WASHING THE WALLS

**1** Paint the walls with two coats of cream-colored latex paint. Mix a glaze using terra-cotta paint and acrylic scumble and brush onto the wall, painting a small area at a time. Before the glaze dries, wipe it with a cloth to give a washed effect.

**2** Plan the pattern using a square of card as a guide before painting the flowers, as shown in the photograph below.

**3** Paint the border using stencil A.

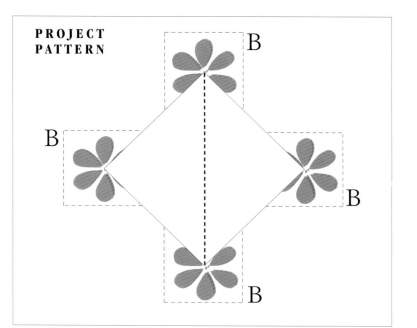

**PROJECT PATTERN**

B    B    B    B

### POSITIONING THE FLOWERS
Mark a vertical line. Cut a square of card and draw a line diagonally across it. Holding the card to the vertical, mark where the corners of the card touch the wall. These will be the flower positions. Mark the whole wall in this way as a guide for your pattern.

### PAINTING THE FLOWERS
Load a sponge with crimson red, remove the excess paint on paper towels, and paint some of the flowers using a dabbing action. Repeat with the other reds, using a new sponge for each color. Paint the centers of the flowers green or gold for contrast.

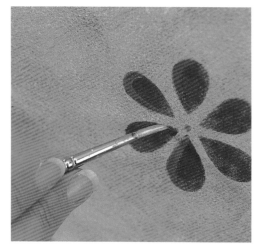

### ADDING GOLD HIGHLIGHTS
Pour a little gold acrylic paint onto a saucer. Using an art brush, pick up some paint and apply it to the edges of the flowers to highlight them. Perfect your technique on paper first.

# INDIAN BLOOMS VARIATIONS

These simple Indian Blooms stencils allow a great deal of flexibility when decorating—you can create borders, wallpapers, and circular motifs. The variety of patterns shown here may inspire you to design many others. Experiment by combining the stencils and using different colors. Try rich, jewel-like hues of deep blue and green, and add touches of gold to enhance particular areas.

**HALF FLOWER AND RIBBON BORDER (STENCILS A AND B)**

**RIBBON EDGING (STENCIL A)**

**LEAF BORDER (STENCIL D)**

**LEAF ROSETTE BORDER (STENCIL D)**

**FLOWER AND LEAVES BORDER (STENCILS B AND C)**

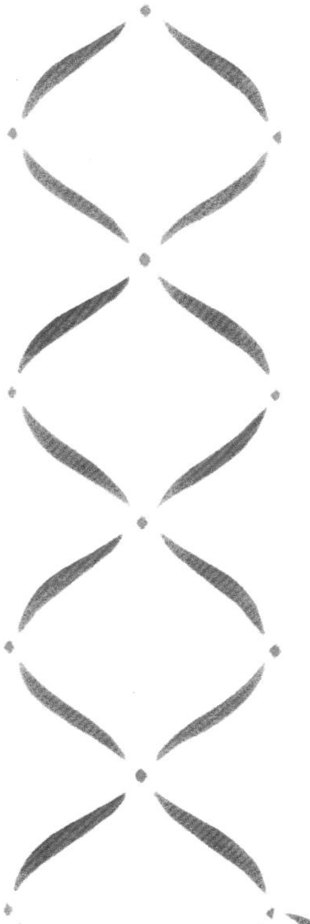

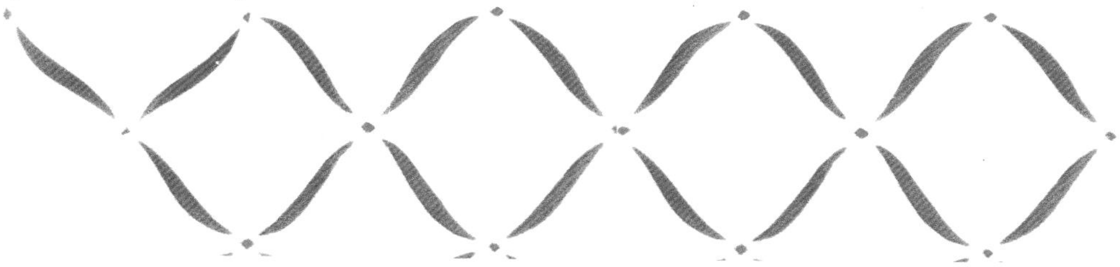

**FLOWER BORDER (STENCIL B)**

**DOUBLE RIBBON BORDER (STENCIL A)**

**LEAVES MOTIF (STENCIL C)**

**FLOWER AND LEAVES ROSETTE
(STENCILS B AND C)**

**DOUBLE FLOWER
MOTIF
(STENCIL B)**

**RIBBONS PATTERN (STENCIL A)**

**LEAF EDGING
(STENCIL C)**

**HALF-FLOWER BORDER (STENCIL B)**

**DOUBLE LEAF BORDER (STENCIL D)**

# SCANDINAVIAN FLOWERS

These Scandinavian-style stencils were inspired by the architectural detail on a 19th-century Swedish house decorated in the Gustavian style. Their charm lies in their simplicity and the wonderful muted colors of the traditional Scandinavian palette. Soft gray-greens and blues combine to make this a very restful room. The border has been created by combining the leaf stencils, and the wall is covered with individual tumbling leaves. To create a completely different look, try painting these stencils in strong, bright colors.

## PAINT COLOR GUIDE

| | | |
|---|---|---|
| Cream | Deep blue-green | Mid-blue-green |
| Pale blue-green | | Blue-gray |

### PLANNING A BORDER

1 Carefully position the individual pieces to make a stylized border. The design here uses the three leaf stencils (C, D, and E) and part of the hanging bells stencil (F).

2 Draw the design on a sheet of paper before you begin and note how the pieces are arranged. This will make it much easier when you come to put them on the wall.

3 Measure the distance to be covered carefully so that the pattern will fit, working each part of the design from its center.

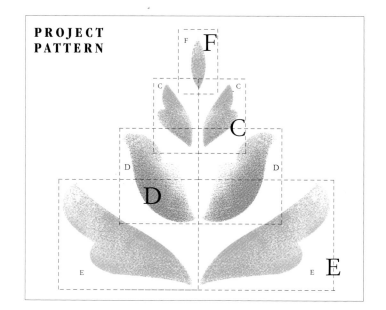

PROJECT PATTERN

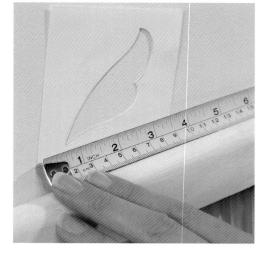

**POSITIONING THE STENCIL**
Mark the center of the wall for the position of the first stencil. Measure the wall and calculate how to fit the complete design without bending the stencils around corners.

**ALIGNING THE STENCILS**
The complete design is formed by painting leaf stencil E, flipping it over, and painting it again as a mirror image, then repeating the process with leaves D and C. This is topped with the drop shape from stencil F. Measure from a central vertical line.

**PAINTING**
Use a sponge for each color. Begin with the lowest leaf, painting in the order blue-gray, dark blue-green, mid-blue-green, and pale blue-green, blending from leaf to leaf. This gives weight and interest to the design.

# SCANDINAVIAN FLOWERS VARIATIONS

**T**ry playing with these stencils to make interesting patterns. You can use just one leaf stencil to create a number of different borders. Flip the stencil over, turn it around, or overlap the images. Use the hearts and leaves to produce a countryside feel; or the "comma," ribbon, and hanging bells for a more formal effect. Subtle color combinations can make simple designs look elegant and sophisticated.

**DOUBLE ROPE BORDER (STENCIL A)**

**LEAF BORDER (STENCIL C)**

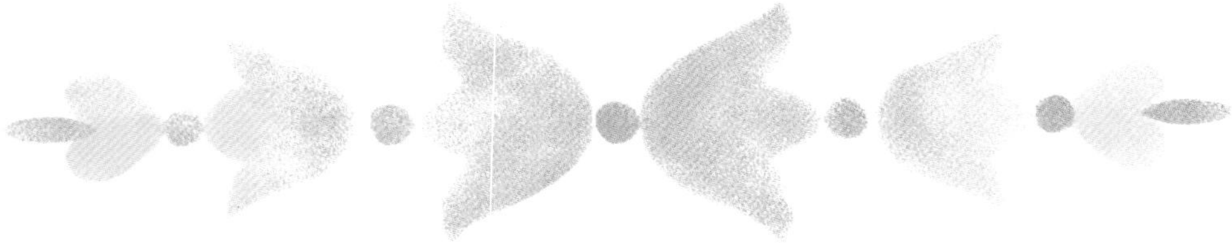

**FLOWERS BORDER (STENCIL F)**

**SCROLL SWIRL (STENCIL B)**

**LEAVES AND HEARTS CIRCLE (STENCILS C AND F)**

**HEARTS POSIES (STENCIL F)**

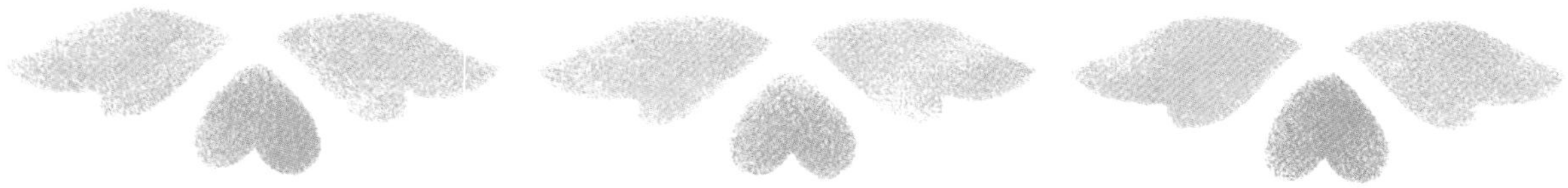

**LEAVES AND HEARTS BORDER (STENCILS C AND F)**

**DOUBLE LEAVES BORDER (STENCIL E)**

**SCROLLS FRAME (STENCIL B)**

**SCROLLS BORDER (STENCIL B)**

**LEAF BORDER (STENCIL C)**

**FLOWERS AND LEAVES BORDER (STENCILS B, C, AND F)**

**OVERLAPPING LEAVES (STENCIL D)**

**ROPE AND FLOWER BORDER (STENCILS A AND F)**

# *rustic* charm

Country life is the theme of this selection of stencils.

These designs celebrate that wholesome world where

nature is honored and where simple charm is preferred

to sophisticated style. The honest appeal of these

patterns gives them a calming air that makes them

perfect for creating a sense of tranquility. From chickens

and ducks to fall berries and traditional herbs, the

designs in this chapter will bring a breath of country air

into your home—wherever you may live.

# FALL HEDGEROW

Capture the richness of fall with these hedgerow stencils of rich, juicy blackberries, ripe rose hips, and leaves changing color from green to russet. This archway decorated with fruit and leaves trailing haphazardly around its frame perfectly evokes the season of "mists and mellow fruitfulness." The stencils are ideal for creating matching, but not identical, designs in other areas of the room. Use random combinations of patterns to paint a border or highlight another feature, such as a window.

## PAINT COLOR GUIDE

| | | |
|---|---|---|
| Yellow ocher | Plum | Bright red |
| Fresh green | Warm yellow | |

### ARRANGING THE STENCILS

1 Arranging these stencils requires a little practice. Start by painting one stencil, perhaps some leaves. Then hold another of the designs to it to decide which section to paint next; choose all or part of a design, whichever looks right in that position.

2 Continue building up your design in this way. The patterns can be made to curve around an arch, make a border, or trail around a corner.

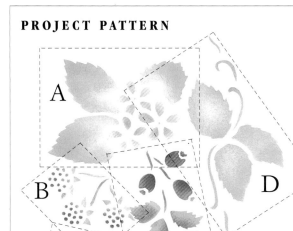

**PROJECT PATTERN**

A

B

C

D

E

### POSITIONING THE STENCILS
Position the stencils individually to curve around the archway. A random arrangement will look more natural than a repetition of the same designs. Start with one of the stencils, adding all or parts of the other designs to form a pleasing arrangement.

### PAINTING THE STENCIL
Paint the blackberries (stencil B) with the plum paint, and the rose hips (stencil E) with bright red. Use yellow and green for the flowers and leaves. Blend and shade colors to enhance the effect. A touch of red on the edge of a leaf works well.

### EXTRA DETAILS
Use parts of the stencil to add extra details and balance the design. A single flower or fruit may be all that is needed. Mask off areas of the stencil that you are not using.

# FALL HEDGEROW VARIATIONS

The look of the hedgerow stencils can be changed by masking some details, and by combining the leaves from one stencil with the flowers from another. Or choose a single motif and repeat it, as shown in the blackberry border. The "triangular" rose hip cluster has one rose hip omitted so that it fits neatly together. Vary the intensity of the colors you use, experiment, and find your own style.

**FLOWER CIRCLET (STENCIL C)**

**FLOWER BORDER (STENCIL C)**

**FLOWER BORDER (STENCILS A AND D)**

**ROSE HIP DROP (STENCIL E)**

**BLACKBERRIES AND LEAVES (STENCILS B, D, AND E)**

**ABOVE: BLACKBERRY CORNER (STENCIL B)**

**ROSE HIP CLUSTER
(STENCIL E)**

**RIGHT: FLOWER SQUARE
(STENCIL A)**

**TRAILING LEAVES BORDER (STENCIL D)**

**BLACKBERRY EDGING (STENCIL B)**

**ROSE HIP BORDER (STENCIL E)**

# DUCKS & CHICKENS LATTICE

**W**arm, rich purple, terra cotta, and earth tones conjure up a cozy farmhouse feel, with ducks and chickens in brilliant gold for a touch of sophistication. These traditional rustic colors immediately suggest a welcoming atmosphere. Just imagine the smell of freshly baked bread wafting through the kitchen and smoking log fires—utter bliss. You can use this project to create a tiled effect, transforming a townhouse kitchen or breakfast room, or to enhance your rural surroundings.

## PAINT COLOR GUIDE

| | |
|---|---|
| Muted purple | Dusky cream |
| Terra cotta | Gold |

### PAINTING A TILED EFFECT

**1** Paint the wall in dark-cream latex to simulate a grout color.

**2** Calculate the size of your tiles. Draw them on the wall, with the aid of a level, leaving a ⅜" (1 cm) gap between each tile.

**3** Divide a roll of masking tape lengthwise using a craft knife so that you have tape ⅜" (1 cm) wide. Stick the tape where you require the grout lines.

**4** Mix latex paint with flat glaze in different shades, then paint the tiles. Remove the tape. You will be left with squares of color.

**5** Stencil the lattice first (stencils E and F) and fill in the round blank space with feathers, ducks, or chickens.

**6** Give the whole surface a couple of layers of varnish.

**PROJECT PATTERN**

The lattice tiles in the photograph opposite are put together as shown here, ready for your choice of motif in the center.

F E F

E E

F E F

### POSITIONING THE LATTICE
To position the lattice (stencils E and F), mark the stencil card with a permanent pen to correspond with the tile lines behind. It does not matter if the stencils are not exactly straight—it will add to the hand-painted look— but it is worth trying to keep them in line.

### APPLYING METALLIC GOLD PAINT
Using a metallic paint is slightly more difficult than using an ordinary paint. You need to apply it more thickly to achieve an opaque look that really shines. Work on two tiles at the same time so that each stage can dry and you do not smudge the work you have just done.

### PAINTING THE BIRDS
To emphasize the gold and to give the chickens and ducks depth, it is a good idea to stencil some of the birds in a dark color first and work on top with gold when dry. This also helps to give the bird shapes a well-defined outer edge.

# DUCKS & CHICKENS LATTICE VARIATIONS

This project seems to suit muted earth tones best, but you could try any combination of colors. The feathers would look especially good in bright hues as an all-over wall design, floating and drifting on the surface. You could stencil the ducks and chickens in regimental rows, or place them randomly as if waddling and pecking around the farmyard.

**QUILLS BORDER (STENCIL D)**

**RIGHT: BIRDS FRIEZE (STENCILS A AND C)**

**LATTICE TILE (STENCIL F)**

**BIRDS AND LATTICE EDGING (STENCILS A, C, AND E)**

**FEATHERS MOTIF (STENCIL D)**

ABOVE: LATTICE
EDGING
(STENCIL E)

LATTICE FRIEZE
(STENCIL E)

FLOATING FEATHERS
(STENCIL B)

ABOVE: CHICKEN
ROUNDELAY
(STENCILS A
AND F)

LATTICE
CORNER
(STENCIL F)

## PAINT COLOR GUIDE

Bright pink          Deep green

Bright yellow

### PAINTING A WALLPAPER DESIGN

1 Paint the background with a coat of yellow latex.

2 The first stripe is a simple 180-degree turn using the same honeysuckle motif (stencil C). Measure the width of the first honeysuckle and use this as the width of your stripe. Use a level to mask off one side of each stripe with low-tack tape, and draw in the alignment of the tape on the stencil so that you can move it up or down easily and accurately.

3 Using the other stencils, repeat the above technique. The gap between the stenciled stripes should be just wider than the stenciling.

# COTTAGE GARDEN

This charming association of flowers, with its glorious cluster of old-fashioned honeysuckle and sweet peas, could be found in any cottage garden. With its profusion of vibrant colors, it lends itself to a bedroom setting. Include the insects—dragonflies, ladybugs, and butterflies—hovering around the gooseberry bushes to capture the rural imagery associated with lazy summer evenings. This stencil could be used in a variety of ways—to enhance bedside tables, bedheads, lampshades, chests of drawers, and mirrors.

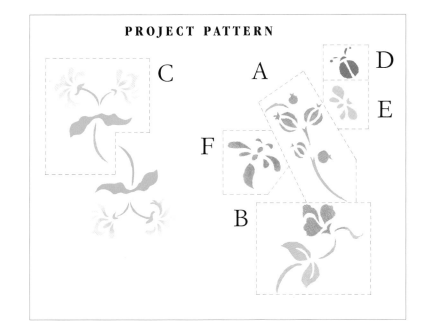

### PROJECT PATTERN

---

#### CHOOSING COLORS
Do not worry if you overlap colors or choose unusual ones—remember that you are working with pattern and shape rather than reality. If you paint an insect green that would normally be blue, it simply adds charm to the stenciling.

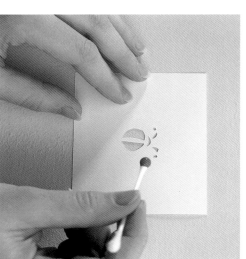

#### PAINTING THE INSECTS
When painting the insect stencils, it is easier to apply the paint with a cotton swab to make sure you do not flood the stencil. Using it like a sponge, dab off the excess paint onto paper towels and then gently work it into the stencil.

#### EXTENDING THE THEME
Stenciling one element in a room with a single pattern can enhance the object and provide a visual link with the stenciled walls. Paint the object in the same way as the walls and protect it with a few layers of varnish.

# COTTAGE GARDEN VARIATIONS

Paint a cottage garden in your bedroom or anywhere else in the house. The simple addition of blue substantially changes the look of these motifs, and you can blend colors to produce realistic-looking fruits. Use them as single images on a variety of objects and furniture, or in combinations to create a country scene as a border or frieze around a room.

**SIMPLE GOOSEBERRY BORDER (STENCIL A)**

**GOOSEBERRIES BORDER (STENCIL A)**

**TRAILING SWEET PEAS REPEAT (STENCIL B)**

**SWEET PEAS, BUTTERFLIES, AND GOOSEBERRIES BORDER (STENCILS A, B, AND E)**

**SWEET PEAS AND INSECTS MOTIF (STENCILS B, E, AND F)**

**ENTWINED SWEET PEAS AND BUTTERFLIES (STENCILS B AND E)**

**GOOSEBERRY AND DRAGONFLY CORNER (STENCILS A AND F)**

**GOOSEBERRIES AND DRAGONFLIES MOTIF (STENCILS A AND F)**

**HONEYSUCKLE BORDER (STENCIL C)**

**RIGHT: HONEYSUCKLE AND DRAGONFLY MOTIF (STENCILS C AND F)**

**TANGLED HONEYSUCKLE AND DRAGONFLIES PATTERN (STENCILS C AND F)**

**HONEYSUCKLE REPEAT (STENCIL C)**

# PAISLEY HARVEST

## PAINT COLOR GUIDE

Plum    Scarlet    Gold

### DECORATING THE WARDROBE

**1** Paint the wardrobe with white latex, then loosely apply a wash of yellow ocher latex and water on top.

**2** The side panel stencil is a simple 180-degree turn of the same shape (stencil A)—once you have stenciled the first image, turn the stencil upside down and position the second. Use a permanent pen to indicate the edge of the previous stencil for an identical repeat.

**3** For the main panel, trace the desired pattern of stencils. Draw the edge of the wardrobe on the tracing so that you can move the pattern down easily. Stick the top edge of the tracing to the wardrobe, and lift it up and down to put the stencils in place.

**T**here is an Indian theme to this design of opulent pears and stylized flowers combined with exotic paisley-shaped leaves. The flowers are loosely based on an Indian jasmine, and the paisley shape is reputed to have originated from Kashmir. The rich colors of deep red, plum, and gold convey the essence of Indian culture. Wood is a suitable surface for this Eastern transformation, and gold, with its jewel-like qualities, serves to enhance the design and highlight the shapes.

Protect your stenciling by applying a good acrylic or polyurethane varnish.

PROJECT PATTERN

A

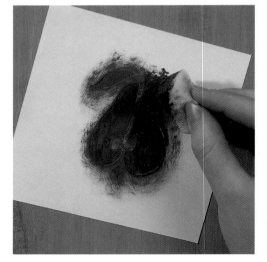

**ADDING DEPTH**
If you want to create a dense layer of paint, do not overflood the stencil in one layer. Aim to build up thin layers of paint until you achieve the required look.

**BRUSHING ON HIGHLIGHTS**
Hand finishing stencils with a brush gives a wonderful individuality to the design. Either leave the stencil on as a guide and outline a shape, or if you are feeling brave, simply paint on the detail.

**SPONGING ON HIGHLIGHTS**
Highlights in metallic paints add instant impact. Wait for the initial coat of paint to dry, then carefully reposition the stencil and work from the outside of the shape, rubbing the sponge gently inward to leave a faded and uneven edge.

# PAISLEY HARVEST VARIATIONS

The wardrobe was decorated with the colors associated with the region of Kashmir—deep reds, plum, and gold—but you could also use the riot of iridescent colors found in Rajasthan. Fuchsia pink, yellow ocher, and scarlet are reminiscent of the festival of Holi, where teenagers shower each other with brilliant red powder dye. So be brave—use bright colors for maximum impact.

If you prefer the more muted look of faded frescoes, use soft hues, gently merging the edges into the background.

ENTWINED LEAF DESIGN (STENCIL A)

SIMPLE LEAF EDGING (STENCIL D)

LARGE PEARS BORDER (STENCIL F)

FLOWER AND SEED HEADS REPEAT (STENCIL C)

SMALL PEARS AND FOLIAGE REPEAT (STENCILS B, D, AND E)

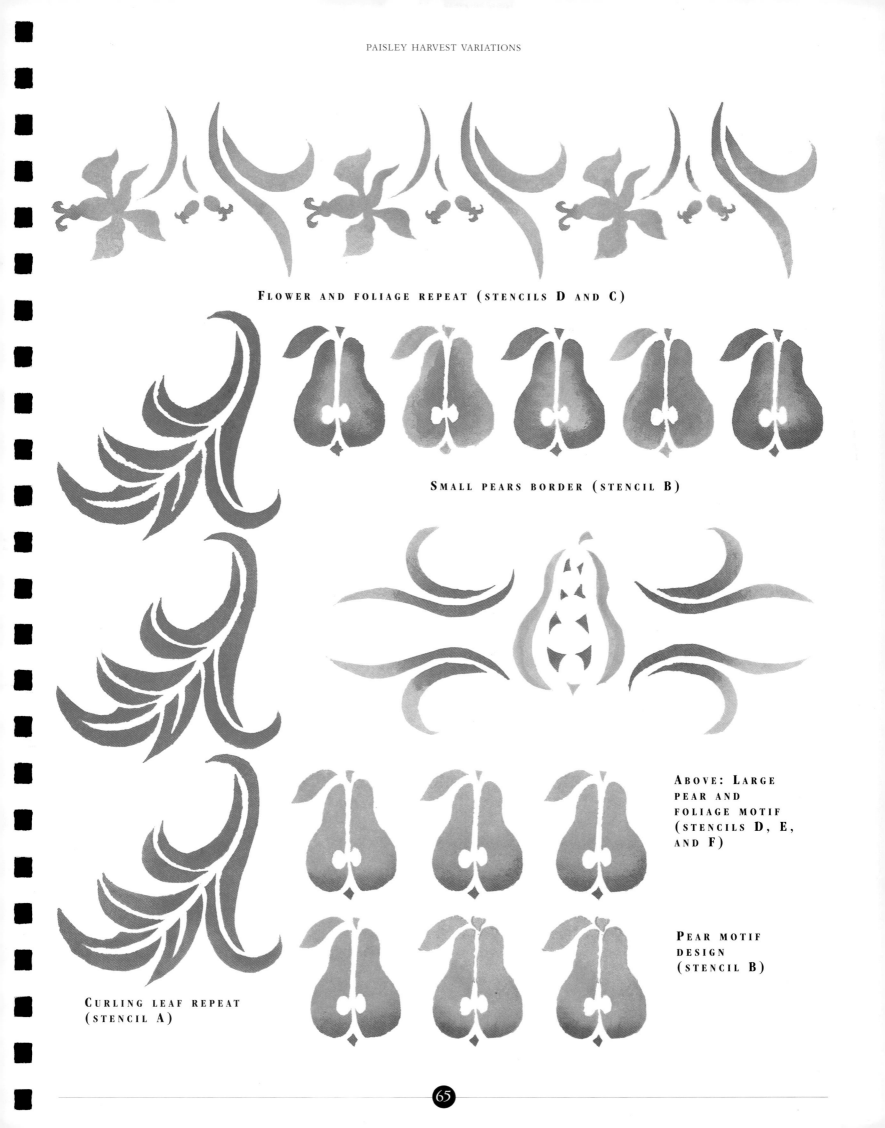

**FLOWER AND FOLIAGE REPEAT (STENCILS D AND C)**

**SMALL PEARS BORDER (STENCIL B)**

**ABOVE: LARGE PEAR AND FOLIAGE MOTIF (STENCILS D, E, AND F)**

**PEAR MOTIF DESIGN (STENCIL B)**

**CURLING LEAF REPEAT (STENCIL A)**

# PATCHWORK TABLECLOTH

Red and white checks seem to conjure up the instant warmth of a farmhouse. With just a few basic shapes, combined at random, it is easy to create a pattern that looks a great deal more complicated than it really is. This project requires patient planning, but the end result is incredibly satisfying—a tablecloth that is crying out for a steaming pot of coffee and copious quantities of homemade cookies to be set upon it.

## PAINT COLOR GUIDE

Bright red     Cream     White

### PAINTING THE TROMPE L'OEIL CLOTH

1 Map out freehand with a faint pencil line where you want the tablecloth to be. If you are working on raw wood, prime it. Paint the base color of the cloth in a cream-colored latex.

2 When dry, load up a paintbrush with the same cream color and paint a ridge on the edge of the cloth. Do this by slightly twisting the brush outward, away from the cloth toward the wood. Paint in a white line to finish the edge.

3 Stencil the solid red square shapes first (stencil G).

4 Fill in the empty squares at random. Stand back regularly to check that the different elements are evenly distributed.

5 Stencil a line of stitches (stencil B) along the outside edge. Finally, varnish the cloth.

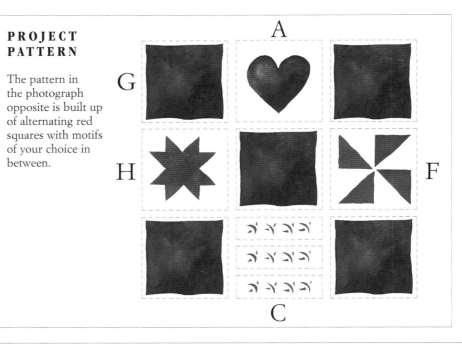

**PROJECT PATTERN**

The pattern in the photograph opposite is built up of alternating red squares with motifs of your choice in between.

A

G

H

F

C

**PAINTING THE EDGE OF THE CLOTH**
To make the cloth look more three-dimensional, paint a ridge on the outside edge and finish it off with a thin white line. This will give the illusion that the cloth is sitting on top of the table rather than painted on.

**MARKING OUT THE SQUARES**
Find the center of the cloth and mark out the first square in pencil by drawing inside stencil G. Draw lines across the square from corner to corner and extend them to the edge of the cloth. Mark 5¼" (13 cm) intervals along these lines. Following the direction of the first square, link the lines together to create a grid, enabling you to position the stencil card easily.

**PLACING THE MOTIFS**
Stencil the nonsymmetrical motifs in all directions so that they can be viewed from all angles. For example, position a heart facing up in one square, down in the next, or to the left or right. Finally, erase any remaining pencil lines and apply a couple of layers of varnish. An oil-based varnish makes the surface slightly heat resistant and gives a yellow tinge, which unifies the whole surface.

# PATCHWORK TABLECLOTH VARIATIONS

**B**y painting the patchwork design in blue and yellow ocher, you can create a softer look, perhaps lifted with just a little red for warmth. An unusual variation would be to paint a wallhanging using the double stitch (stencil D) as fringing. The motifs can be used to give impact in small areas, or in more muted shades to create a Shaker-style design.

**SQUARE AND HEART MOTIF (STENCILS A AND G)**

**BELOW: STITCHED HEART BORDER (STENCILS A AND D)**

**ABOVE: STAR TILES (STENCIL H)**

**RIGHT: HEARTS STRIPES (STENCILS A AND C)**

**LEFT: SQUARE AND WINDMILL BLOCKS (STENCILS F AND G)**

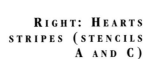

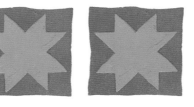

**STAR AND STITCH BORDER (STENCILS B, G, AND H)**

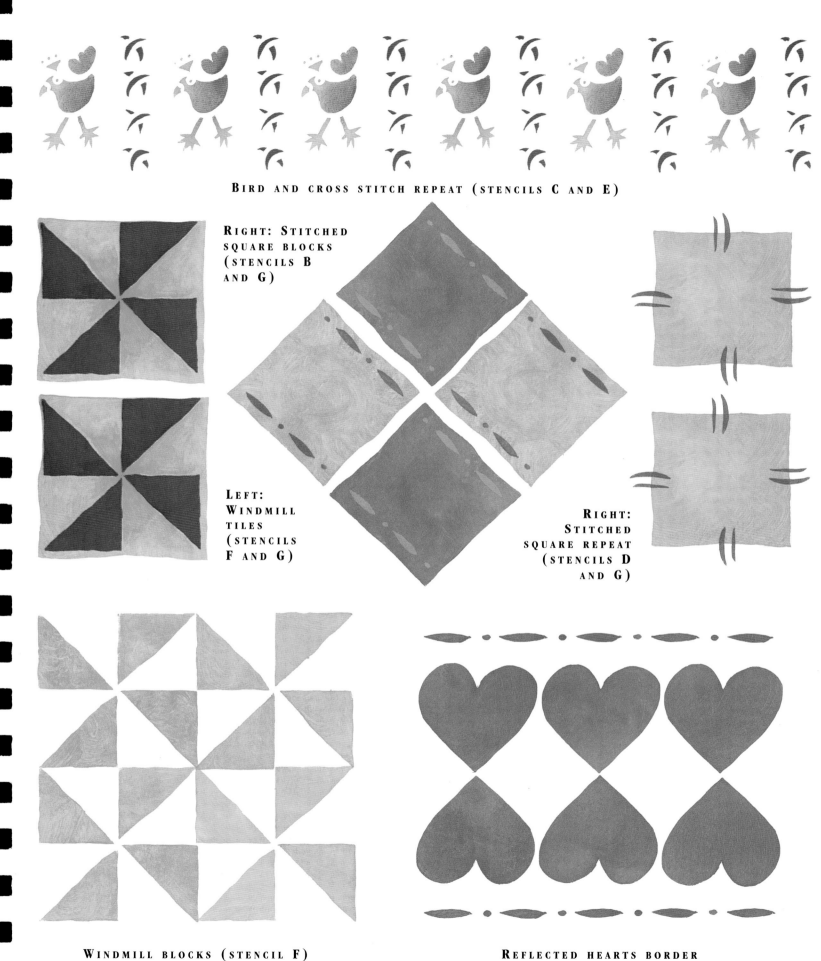

**BIRD AND CROSS STITCH REPEAT (STENCILS C AND E)**

**RIGHT: STITCHED SQUARE BLOCKS (STENCILS B AND G)**

**LEFT: WINDMILL TILES (STENCILS F AND G)**

**RIGHT: STITCHED SQUARE REPEAT (STENCILS D AND G)**

**WINDMILL BLOCKS (STENCIL F)**

**REFLECTED HEARTS BORDER (STENCILS A AND B)**

# TULIPS & CHICKEN WIRE

A lime-green color wash and tulips in bright pink and green give this storage cupboard a more contemporary look. Painting the chicken wire silver keeps the metallic feel, while a light wash of yellow ocher as a ground for the tulip design maintains the rustic character. By positioning the tulips haphazardly on the cupboard, you can imagine the kitchen door blowing open and the wind moving the flowers around, before someone shuts out the cold air and the room becomes a warm haven once more.

## PAINT COLOR GUIDE

| | | |
|---|---|---|
| Lime green | Yellow ocher | Cream |
| Bright pink | Silver | |

### PAINTING A STORAGE CUPBOARD

**1** Apply a coat of primer to raw wood, then paint with cream latex.

**2** Apply a lime-colored wash to the outside areas and an ocher wash to the stencil background. The washes should consist of latex paint diluted with water.

**3** Paint the chicken wire (stencil A) using silver metallic paint. Stencil petals (B, D, and E) in a haphazard arrangement, then complete with the leaves (stencil F).

**4** Finally, coat the whole surface with two layers of water-based varnish.

### PROJECT PATTERN

This arrangement shows just one of the patterns used on the cupboard in the photograph opposite.

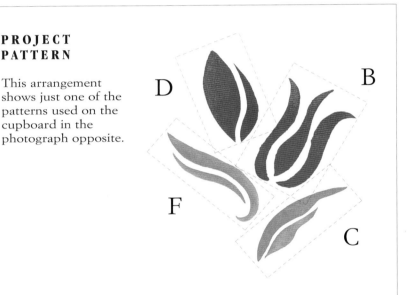

**PLACING THE MOTIFS**
With a dark pen, draw around the outside edge of each stencil motif onto paper. Cut around this line drawing, following the shape exactly. Repeat the process a few times for each motif until you have sufficient to build up your pattern. Stick the paper cutouts in the required positions with spray adhesive.

**PAINTING THE CHICKEN WIRE DESIGN**
Stencil across the surface with chicken wire (stencil A), painting right over the paper shapes. Wait for it to dry completely and then carefully peel off the paper. Peel one shape at a time so that you leave a clean outline.

**ADDING THE TULIPS**
Once the paper cutouts are peeled off, the clear negative spaces will be revealed. Lay the stencil cards on top of the negative spaces and stencil the tulips in bright pink, bringing the project to life. Using the same technique, paint the leaves in bright green.

# TULIPS & CHICKEN WIRE VARIATIONS

The chicken wire design looks equally effective as a background pattern or worked over the top of the other stencils. You could even experiment with tulips growing in and out of the wire. The flowers can be painted in bold, bright colors or in soft, pastel shades, and like any garden planting, they look good in a variety of combinations. Experimentation is the key, and the shapes can be used in a stylized rather than natural manner if you wish.

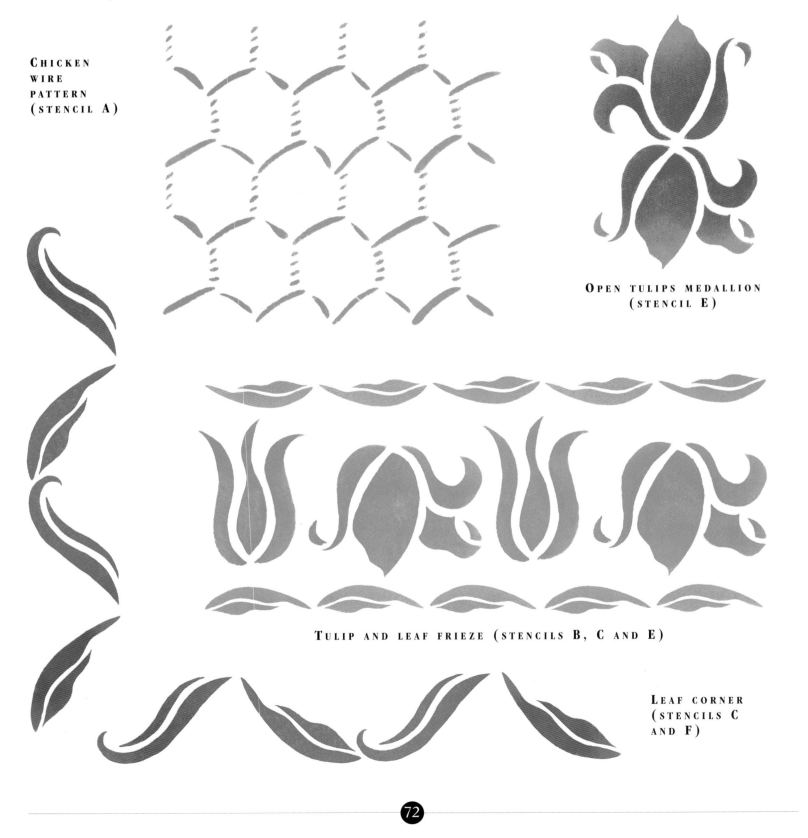

CHICKEN
WIRE
PATTERN
(STENCIL A)

OPEN TULIPS MEDALLION
(STENCIL E)

TULIP AND LEAF FRIEZE (STENCILS B, C AND E)

LEAF CORNER
(STENCILS C
AND F)

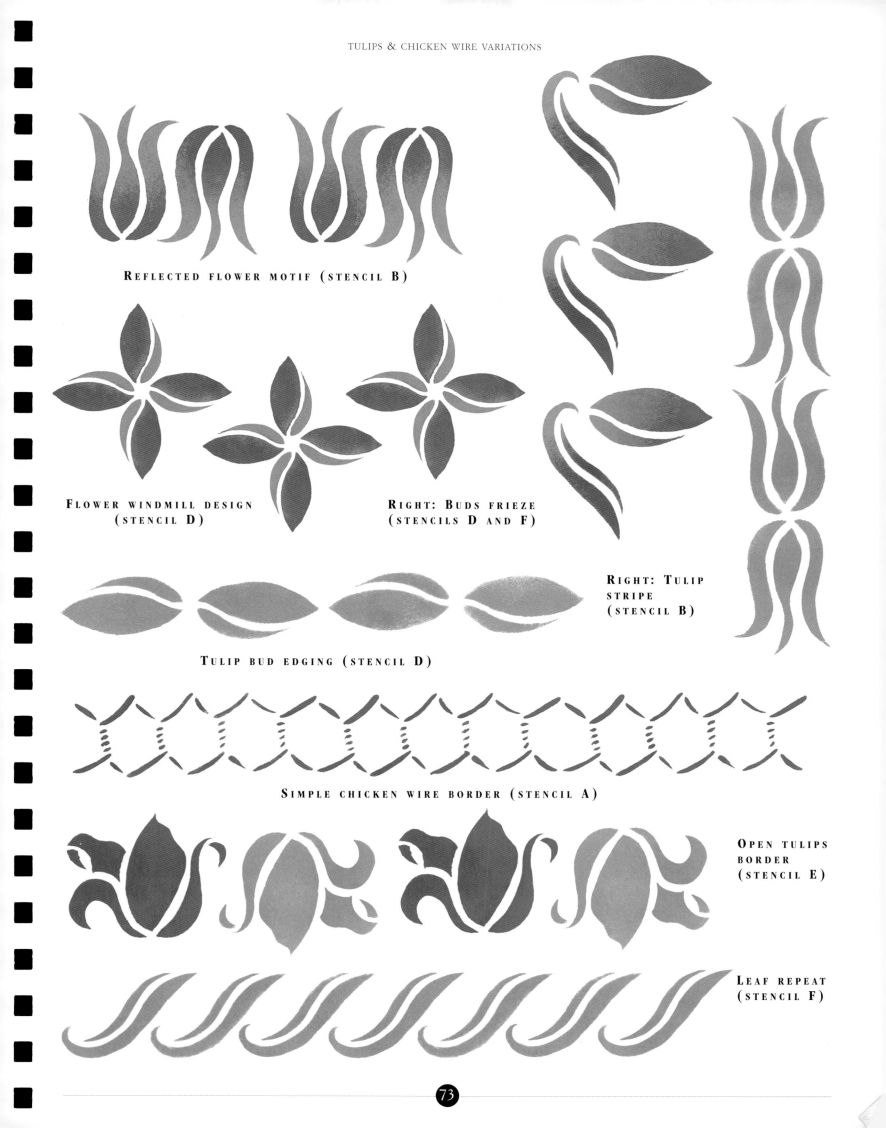

**REFLECTED FLOWER MOTIF (STENCIL B)**

**FLOWER WINDMILL DESIGN (STENCIL D)**

**RIGHT: BUDS FRIEZE (STENCILS D AND F)**

**TULIP BUD EDGING (STENCIL D)**

**RIGHT: TULIP STRIPE (STENCIL B)**

**SIMPLE CHICKEN WIRE BORDER (STENCIL A)**

**OPEN TULIPS BORDER (STENCIL E)**

**LEAF REPEAT (STENCIL F)**

## PAINT COLOR GUIDE

Cream      Sage green

Cornflower blue      Purple

### DECORATING THE PLATTER

1 Paint the wooden plate with primer and then with a coat of cream latex.

2 Mix a small amount of sage-green latex with flat glaze, then apply this wash to the plate using big, sweeping movements.

3 Start the stenciling with the ribbon (stencil A) and build up the herbs from the bottom. Fill any gaps with sections of the stencils.

4 Use different gradations of color to give variation and depth to the design.

5 Work your way around the perimeter of the plate, then finish with a couple of layers of varnish to protect your stenciling.

# HERBS & RIBBON

The calm, muted colors of sage green, clear blue, and purple are ideal for creating a gentle, rustic theme. Freshly gathered herbs tied together in bunches with a colorful purple ribbon and hanging from the kitchen beams to dry, conjure up the essence of country life. Sage, rosemary, and thyme are all plants stored for use during the winter months for culinary purposes or herbal remedies, lotions, and potions. Here, they decorate the shelves and a wooden platter.

### PROJECT PATTERN

The border on the plate in the photograph opposite is a simple repeat of this pattern; stencils are superimposed in a random manner to create the bunch of herbs in the center.

F      E

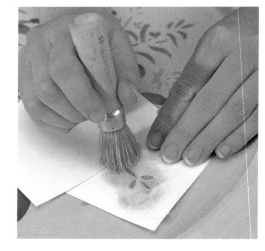

**MASKING OFF PARTS OF STENCILS**
Build up the design as you work, sometimes using the whole shape of the stencil and sometimes masking off sections to fill in the gaps. Do not worry if shapes overlap—it adds to the end result and makes the bunch of herbs look more generous.

**MEASURING FOR THE BORDER**
To have a set repeat around the outside of the plate, first measure the design you want to use, then measure the space you want it to fit into. Divide the plate's circumference by the design length, then mark this on the plate faintly in pencil as a guide.

**GRADUATING COLOR FOR DEPTH**
By graduating the paint color from light to dark within the stencil and repeating this in each subsequent shape, you can achieve an undulating effect. This will give your design more visual movement.

# HERB & RIBBON VARIATIONS

Sage green is a color that seems instantly to suggest a country kitchen, but a much brighter blue-green is used here to good effect. The shape of the thyme sprigs allows them to be trailed wherever you wish, and although the rosemary and sage are slightly more rigid in pattern, they can also be placed in a multitude of designs. Bunches of herbs would look great stenciled as if hanging just below the ceiling.

**REFLECTED STALK FRIEZE (STENCIL C)**

**RIGHT: TWISTED THYME BORDER (STENCIL E)**

**SAGE LEAF EDGING (STENCIL D)**

**ENTWINED RIBBONS BORDER (STENCIL A)**

**ABOVE: RIBBON EDGING (STENCIL A)**

**SAGE LEAF BORDER (STENCIL D)**

**LEFT: REFLECTED STALK EDGING (STENCIL C)**

**ABOVE: SAGE LEAF PATTERN (STENCIL D)**

**RIGHT: LOOPED RIBBON BOW (STENCIL A)**

**ABOVE: ROSEMARY BORDER (STENCIL B)**

**THYME SWAG (STENCIL F)**

**RANDOM RIBBONS (STENCIL A)**

**THYME CIRCLE (STENCIL F)**

# FRITILLARY

Growing these majestic plants from seed can take seven years, so finding them in the wild is a real treat. When I was young, I found a clump growing in a place only reachable by crawling under the prickly bushes at the end of my grandmother's garden. I thought I was the only person to have discovered them, and guarded the secret closely. Years later I discovered that my grandmother had always admired their checkerboard petals and had especially kept that corner of the garden wild.

## PAINT COLOR GUIDE

Olive green    Dark forest green    Burgundy

White    Light terra cotta

### PAINTING THE WALLS AND DRAPE

**1** First, paint the walls in yellow latex. Then add a wash of rich terra cotta. The paint dries quickly and can look patchy if you are not careful, so work fast. It is easier if two people work together.

**2** Plan the entire design on paper and stick it to the wall to see the effect. This also helps you to tackle the corners, and to figure out joins and where the flowers will stop before stenciling them.

**3** The cream voile drape is stenciled with white fabric paint. Put thick paper underneath the fabric and place paint pots on top to keep the stencil in place. Do not move the voile until the paint is dry.

### PROJECT PATTERN

To make the repeat, build up two plants with leaves and flowers. Cut a reverse stencil of A to balance the composition of the stencil group.

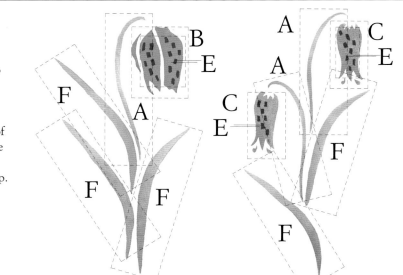

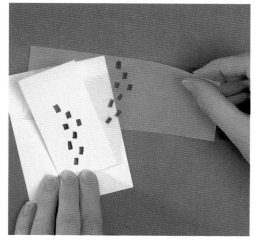

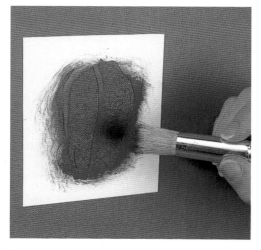

### GRADUATING COLOR BY STIPPLING

You can create movement in your design by using gradations of a single color. Here, white is stippled on gently at first, and then stronger white stippling is added on one side to give a more rounded quality.

### ACHIEVING THE CHECKERBOARD

It can be difficult to get the checkerboard effect in the right position. Trace the squares (stencil E) and their relation to the petals (stencil B) and use this drawing as a guide. Put the tracing in place and match the stencil to it, then remove the tracing.

### ADDING TRANSLUCENCY

If you are using water-based paint and you want your colors to have a more transparent look, try adding a little acrylic glaze to the paint. The glaze will help you spread the paint, producing a more translucent effect.

# FRITILLARY VARIATIONS

F rescoes were traditionally painted directly onto freshly applied terra-cotta plasterwork. You can use solid colors, or fade the colors at the edges so that the pattern is only a faint image with an aged or weathered appearance. Create a timeless quality by omitting some parts. This pattern also lends itself to geometric interpretation, working from the checkerboard pattern on the bloom to achieve symmetry.

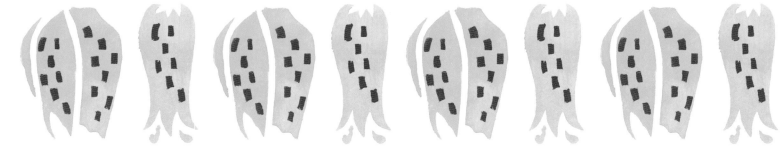

**LEAF REPEAT (STENCIL F)**

**FLOWER HEADS (STENCILS B AND E, AND C AND E)**

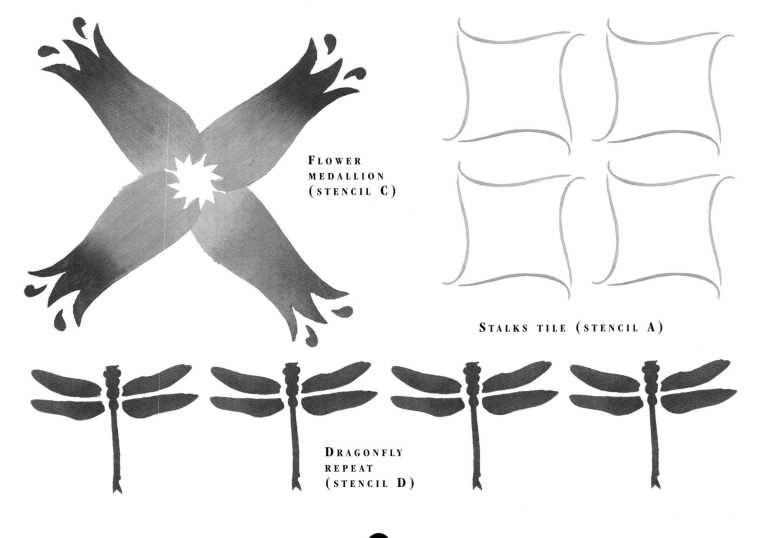

**FLOWER MEDALLION (STENCIL C)**

**STALKS TILE (STENCIL A)**

**DRAGONFLY REPEAT (STENCIL D)**

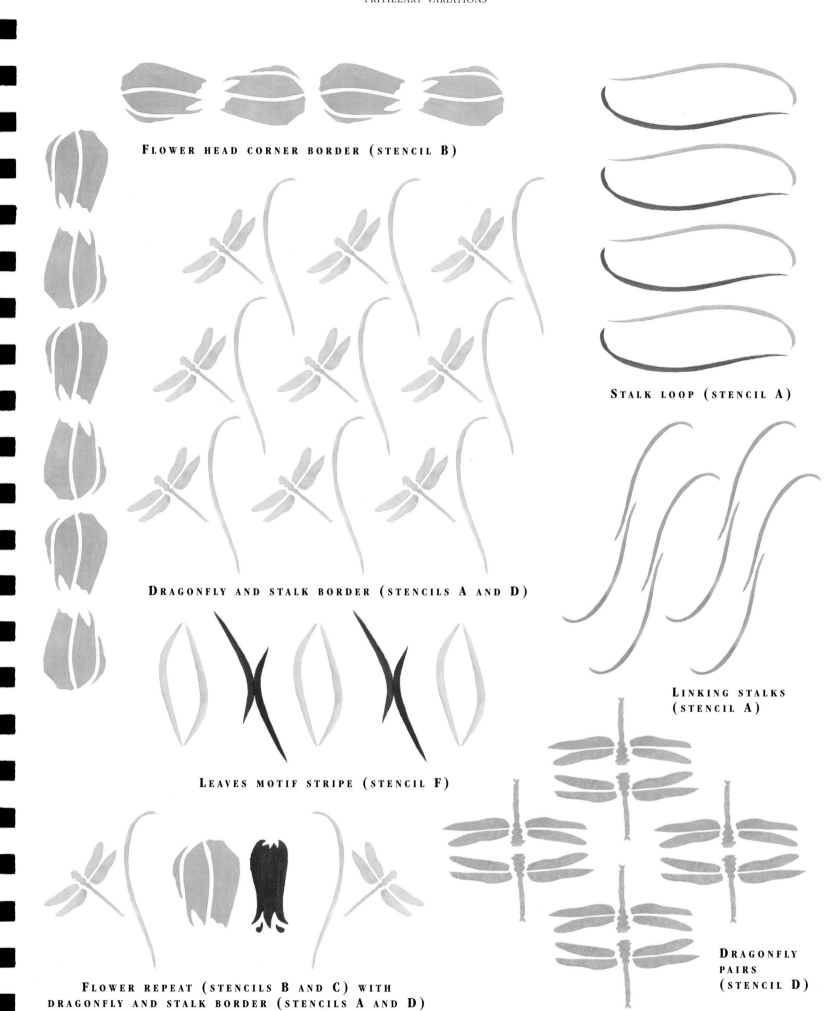

**FLOWER HEAD CORNER BORDER (STENCIL B)**

**STALK LOOP (STENCIL A)**

**DRAGONFLY AND STALK BORDER (STENCILS A AND D)**

**LINKING STALKS
(STENCIL A)**

**LEAVES MOTIF STRIPE (STENCIL F)**

**FLOWER REPEAT (STENCILS B AND C) WITH
DRAGONFLY AND STALK BORDER (STENCILS A AND D)**

**DRAGONFLY
PAIRS
(STENCIL D)**

# nature's harvest

*These designs celebrate the abundance of nature. The many different forms of fruits and flowers give designers a wonderful range of shapes, textures, and colors to experiment with. Try a Mediterranean feel with a Tuscan olive pattern, or a touch of France with Provençal figs and clematis. Closer to home, how about carrots and radishes, or the freshness of peas and beans in the pod. Whatever the room, you're sure to find a pattern for it among these glorious shapes.*

## PAINT COLOR GUIDE

White    Lime green    Dark green

### PAINTING THE BORDER

1 First, paint your wall with a coat of apple-green latex.

2 Carefully mark out the border using a level, then mask off the stenciling area with low-tack tape or string pinned at intervals.

3 Gently spray the backs of the stencils with spray adhesive, set them aside for a few minutes so the glue is not too sticky, then start to put them in position.

4 Position your stencils randomly, trying not to repeat the same motif next to itself. Place them at various angles—even sidewise or upside down. Reposition them until you are happy with the pattern.

# SPRING LILIES & CRAB APPLES

D elicate white lilies are traditionally associated with modesty and purity, but they make an effective contrast with the familiar culinary properties of acid-green crab apples. To create an instant impression of peace and harmony, you could use any of these stencils in different combinations. There are no hard-and-fast rules, so move the stencils as your space dictates. Transform a plain kitchen wall, as here, or perhaps trail the shapes over your garden furniture and containers.

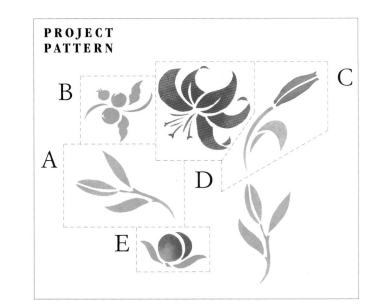

**PROJECT PATTERN**

### PAINTING LIGHT ON DARK
It is usual to start with a light background and paint darker colored stencils onto it. Here, the combination of light on dark and dark on light adds to the depth of the design. To work with white, always use a clean sponge and dry stencil.

### FADING FOR AN AGED LOOK
A fresco effect can be achieved by fading colors into the background. In this way, the end result will not seem contrived, and the stenciled image will look as if it has been on the wall for years.

### BALANCING THE DESIGN
Placing the stencils randomly may sound easy, but it requires careful planning. Stand back at regular intervals to check that the visual weight of the design is even. Experiment with the different elements in any empty spaces until you find one that fits.

# SPRING LILIES & CRAB APPLES VARIATIONS

Instead of the cool effect of the lime-green and white combination used on the kitchen wall, try a variation. How about burgundy lilies with muted green crab apples, for example? Use the lilies on their own or leave the crab apples cooking in rows. For a more sophisticated setting, try the designs in a dining room.

LILY FLOWERS BORDER (STENCIL **D**)

CRAB APPLE FRIEZE IN TWO COLORS (STENCIL **B**)

ONE-TONE BUD AND SPRIG REPEAT (STENCILS **A** AND **C**)

LILY FLOWER AND CRAB APPLE BORDER (STENCILS **B** AND **D**)

CRAB APPLES AND LILY BUD BORDER (STENCILS **A**, **B**, AND **E**)

**LEFT: SIMPLE LINKING SPRIGS (STENCIL C)**

**ABOVE: LARGE CRAB APPLE BORDER (STENCIL E)**

**LEFT: TWISTING CRAB APPLE FRIEZE (STENCIL B)**

**BOLD FLOWER PATTERN (STENCIL D)**

**LILY ART DECO DESIGN (STENCIL C)**

**LILY FLOWER AND BUD REPEAT (STENCILS A AND D)**

**SIMPLE LINKING BUDS (STENCIL A)**

# PROVENÇAL FIGS & CLEMATIS

The balmy atmosphere of the South of France is conjured up by this attractive combination of luscious figs with the stately appearance of large clematis blooms. Earthy colors of dark terra cotta, purple, olive, and cream epitomize fall in Provence. Create a warm and rustic look on anything from chests and kitchen cabinets to archways and study walls. The trailing nature of the clematis plant, with its star-shaped flowers and entwining tendrils, particularly lends itself to floors.

## PAINT COLOR GUIDE

Deep purple          Terra cotta

Olive green          Golden cream

Dark brown

### PAINTING THE FLOOR PATTERN

1 First, whitewash the floorboards with a 50:50 mix of water and white latex. Build up the wash in layers until you have the desired effect.

2 Position the stencil cards on the floor. Try to keep the pattern looking as if it is growing naturally and engulfing the surface.

3 Alternate the leaves with tendrils, flowers, and figs at random. If you come across a good combination, repeat it, but at a good distance from the first so that you achieve a natural-looking effect. Floors should be finished with a couple of coats of varnish.

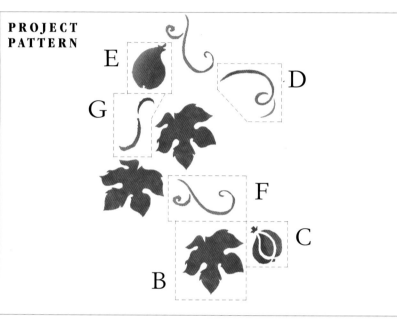

**PROJECT PATTERN**

### MOTTLED LEAVES
To achieve a mottled look within each element, dab the stencil with one color, let it dry for a moment, then sponge a different color on top. This gives a wonderful uneven effect.

### SHADING THE FIGS
Create graduated shading by blending into the first color while it is still wet. Start with the darker color, but do not put it quite as far as you ultimately want the shading to go. Then work back toward this with the lighter color.

### TACKLING CORNERS
Work around corners in as flowing a manner as possible. Sometimes it helps to put an element such as a tendril in the corner to give definition. Stand back as you progress to check you are maintaining the feeling of movement.

# PROVENÇAL FIGS & CLEMATIS VARIATIONS

As a contrast to the ripening purple figs used as a floor decoration, try a more subdued color scheme. For a lighter effect, combine olive-green figs with creamy white clematis blooms. Perhaps you could paint the design growing along the floor, over the baseboard, and up the wall. The motifs could also be used as all-over hand-painted "wallpaper" designs.

**FIGS AND TENDRILS BORDER (STENCILS C AND F)**

**LEAF BLOCK BORDER (STENCIL B)**

**LEFT: SIMPLE RIBBON REPEAT (STENCIL G)**

**CLEMATIS REPEAT (STENCIL A)**

**CLEMATIS AND CURLING TENDRILS BORDER (STENCILS A AND D)**

**SIMPLE FIG BORDER (STENCIL E)**

**TENDRIL EDGING (STENCIL F)**

**LEAF, RIBBON, AND FIG PATTERN (STENCILS B, C, AND G)**

**FIGS AND CURLING TENDRILS (STENCILS C, D, AND E)**

**TENDRIL REPEAT (STENCIL F)**

**FIG BORDER (STENCIL C)**

**TUMBLING LEAVES (STENCIL B)**

**CLEMATIS FLOWER BORDER (STENCILS A AND G)**

# TUSCAN OLIVES

Enjoy long summer evenings sharing a meal with friends around this patio table. Stenciled with plump Mediterranean olives, it brings the flavor and atmosphere of Tuscany to your home. The table is painted in traditional Tuscan earth colors, which are rich and warm, and provide an authentic-looking background for the border of olives. It has been finished with an antiquing varnish that enhances the colors and give the table an aged look. A final coat of clear varnish protects the surface.

## PAINT COLOR GUIDE

| | | |
|---|---|---|
| Mustard yellow | Terra cotta | Olive green |
| Yellow-green | Dark green | Brown |
| Black | | |

### PREPARING AND FINISHING THE TABLE

**1** Paint the table with two coats of mustard-yellow latex paint. Make a glaze using acrylic scumble and terra-cotta paint. Using a soft cloth, pick up some glaze and rub it over the tabletop to give it a textured finish. The base color should now show through the glaze. After stenciling, apply antiquing varnish.

**2** Plan the positions of the stencils by measuring carefully. Design a one-eighth segment around the table to check the fit.

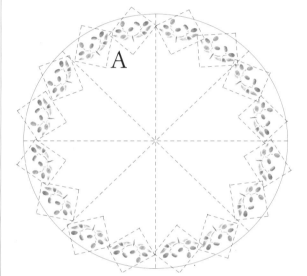

**PROJECT PATTERN**

A

**POSITIONING THE OLIVE STENCIL**
Plan the positions of your stencils around the edge of the tabletop. Measure carefully to be sure that you will not be left with too much or too little space to complete the circle. First, see how a one-eighth segment will look.

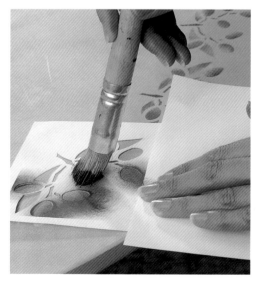

**PAINTING THE OLIVES**
Use a different brush for each color. Load the tip of the brush, remove excess paint on paper towels, then apply the paint by tapping, or "pouncing." For a smoother look, press lightly on the bristles and use a circular motion.

**SHADING**
Solid blocks of color will appear flat and heavy, so highlight one side of each olive with lighter green paint, making the olives appear round. Use two greens on the leaves to give a more realistic effect.

# TUSCAN OLIVES VARIATIONS

Use a single stencil to make a repeating border, or combine parts of the designs for a geometric all-over pattern. To make a square tile design, paint the line stencil as a frame using the ends as a link. Position the leaf stencils inside some of the squares. The variations illustrated here show how the use of color can produce different effects.

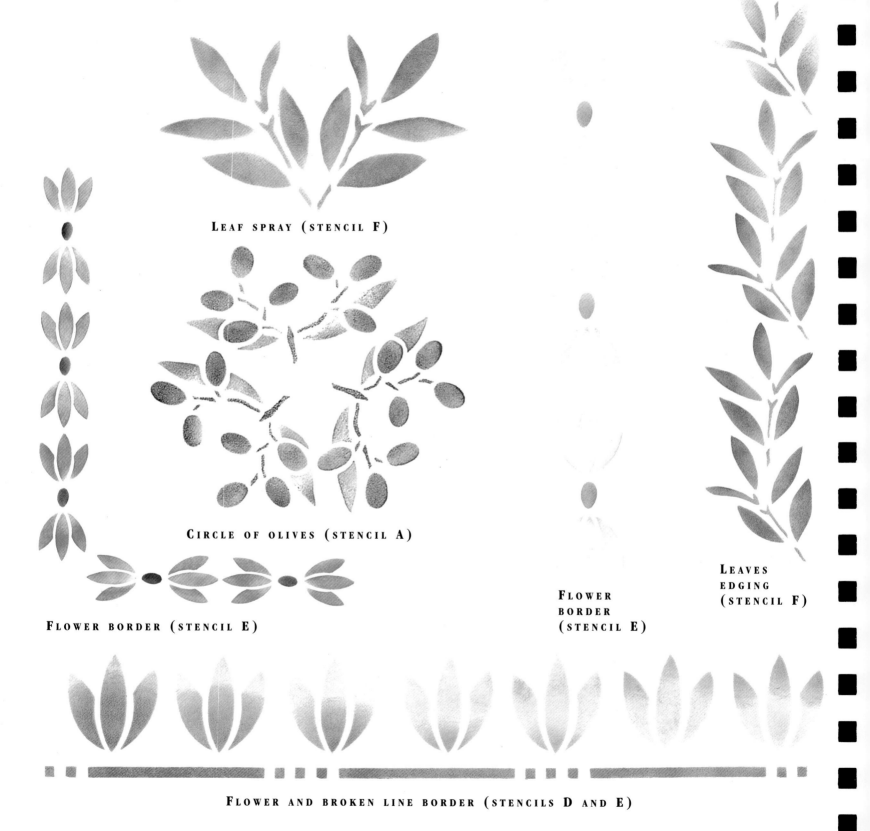

**LEAF SPRAY (STENCIL F)**

**CIRCLE OF OLIVES (STENCIL A)**

**FLOWER BORDER (STENCIL E)**

**FLOWER BORDER (STENCIL E)**

**LEAVES EDGING (STENCIL F)**

**FLOWER AND BROKEN LINE BORDER (STENCILS D AND E)**

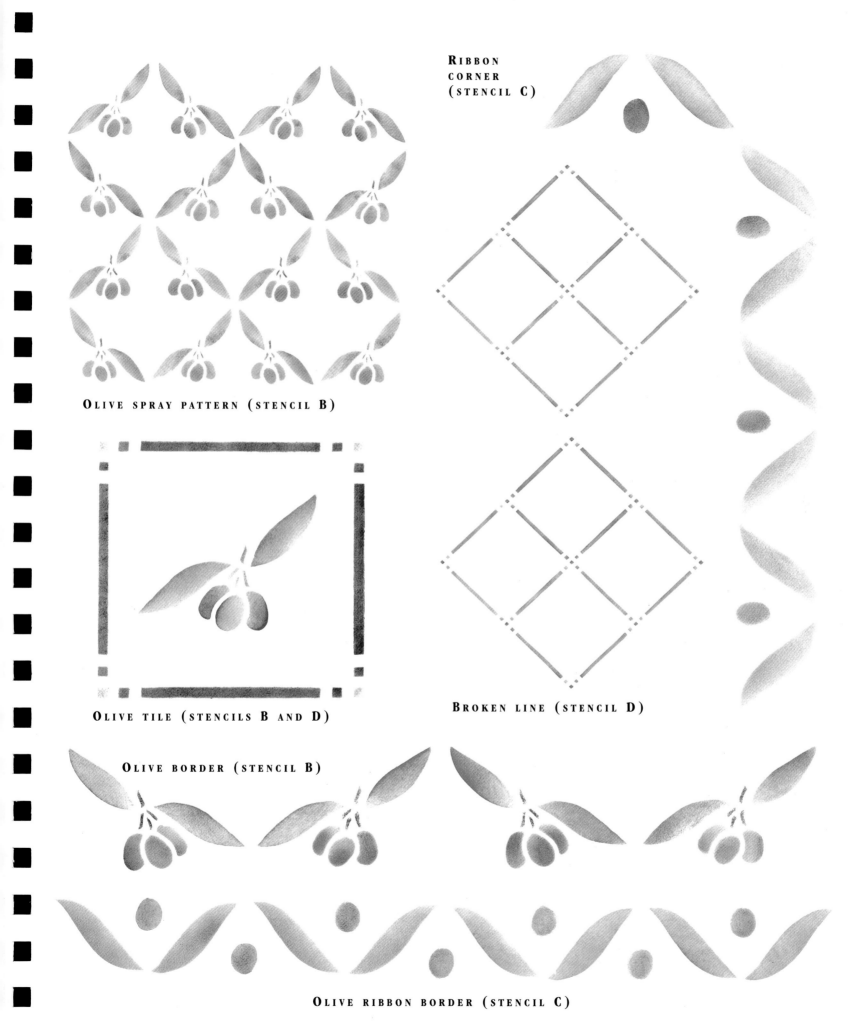

**RIBBON CORNER (STENCIL C)**

**OLIVE SPRAY PATTERN (STENCIL B)**

**OLIVE TILE (STENCILS B AND D)**

**BROKEN LINE (STENCIL D)**

**OLIVE BORDER (STENCIL B)**

**OLIVE RIBBON BORDER (STENCIL C)**

# CARROTS & RADISHES

The clean, crisp, crunchy-looking vegetables in this project seem realistic enough to eat. Spiky topped carrots are combined with round radishes, all looking as if they have just been dug up, had the earth shaken from them, and been washed in freezing cold water. Dark red, bright orange, and lime green are used for a bold effect. The design works best if positioned halfway up the wall, or at the top to form arches that seem to dangle from the ceiling.

## PAINT COLOR GUIDE

Bright orange    Lime green    Dark green

Deep red    Cream

### PAINTING A WALL FRIEZE

1 Coat the wall in an off-white latex paint, then give it a washed look using cream latex mixed with water and water-based flat glaze.

2 Draw a very faint line using a level as a guide to position the stencils. Paint the carrot and radish stencils alternately.

3 When the design is dry, give the whole wall a coat of water-based satin varnish to protect it from the grease and grime of everyday wear and tear. Satin varnish is more practical in the kitchen than a flat one because it repels condensation, steam, and dirt.

### PROJECT PATTERN

This arrangement forms the basis of the repeat pattern on the wall in the photograph opposite.

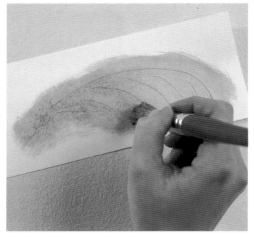

**BLENDING THE LEAF COLORS**
To keep colors from merging within a single shape, work first with one color from one end of the shape. Then use a separate brush to work a second color from the other end toward the first color. Keep a brush solely for blending, and clean the mixing brush on paper towels between each use to blend the colors cleanly.

**GIVING DIMENSION TO THE SHAPES**
The radishes will look more realistic if you paint around the outside of the shape with a swirling motion, leaving a touch of the background color showing in one area as a highlight. Do not worry if you apply the paint heavily in areas—you can overpaint the mistake with the background color.

**STIPPLING THE LEAVES**
A stippled effect can enhance the look of a project like this, giving it more visual movement. Stencil a shape and wait for it to dry. Then take a clean brush with very little paint on it and dab the paint gently over the existing color.

# CARROTS & RADISHES VARIATIONS

**T**hese carrots and radishes can be arranged in many ways as well as in the form of a frieze. Why not paint bunches of carrots hanging like strings of onions? Experiment with different combinations on paper before you start work on a project and plan the positions of the shapes carefully. There is nothing more frustrating than wishing one element was slightly to the left or not there at all.

**CARROT TOP STRIPES (STENCIL D)**

**RIGHT: CARROT CRACKER (STENCILS A AND D)**

**RADISH LEAVES FRIEZE (STENCILS F AND G)**

**RADISH ROOTS PYRAMID (STENCIL E)**

**RADISH LEAF BORDER (STENCIL H)**

**ABOVE: CARROT TOPS BORDER (STENCILS B AND C)**

**ABOVE: RADISH LEAVES CIRCLES (STENCILS F AND G)**

**CARROT TOP PATTERN (STENCIL D)**

**RIGHT: CURVING CARROT TOPS MOTIFS (STENCILS B AND C)**

**CARROT TOPS FRIEZE (STENCIL B)**

**RADISHES AND SPIKY LEAVES BORDER (STENCILS D AND E)**

# PASSION FRUIT & FLOWERS

Here is an easy way to transform an uninteresting flat wall or hallway. Simply divide it along the traditional chair rail position with a stenciled border. Paint the two areas in contrasting tones to create a wonderful backdrop for these rambling, elegant passion fruit and flowers in lilac, green, and burgundy. These motifs look just as effective when applied in a random manner rather than regularly repeated, giving the finished image a more individual, hand-painted look.

## PAINT COLOR GUIDE

Olive green    Lilac    Burgundy

### PAINTING A BORDER DESIGN

1 Paint the top of the wall in a light stone color. Use a level to place a horizontal line of low-tack masking tape along the wall, then paint the lower half in a darker color.

2 Position the two leaf motifs (stencils A and C) so that they overlap the two colors.

3 Finally, put in the flower (stencil D) and fruit (stencil B). This can be done by eye or by drawing in the edge of the previous stencil on the card that you are using to calculate the exact repeat position.

### PROJECT PATTERN

A          D

B          C

**POSITIONING THE REPEAT**
When you first position your stencil, draw a line on the stencil with a permanent pen to indicate where the stencil crosses the dividing line on the wall. This will make the repeat easier to align.

**PAINTING THE LEAVES**
Keep some of the leaves pure green, and add tinges of different colors to the corners of other leaves to produce a more flowing feel.

**PROTECTING THE SURFACE**
You could also paint the stencil with the dark color on top of the light section of wall, and vice versa. If your stencil goes over both backgrounds, put a piece of card on one half for protection and then paint. Repeat the process on the second half.

# PASSION FRUIT & FLOWERS VARIATIONS

Experiment with earthy, fall colors as an alternative to the fresh, summery tones used for the border decoration. With their tendrils and abundant fruits and flowers, these passion fruit stencils can be used to create a "growing" image. Make sure that you undulate the stencils to maintain the sense of movement. Blend the tints of the ripening fruit or keep to a single color.

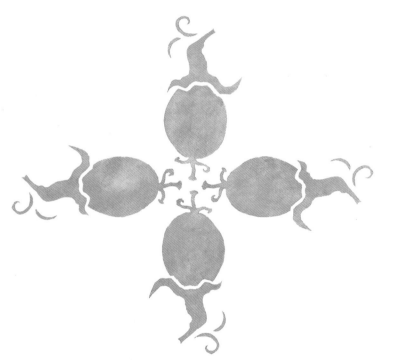

FRUIT MEDALLION DESIGN (STENCIL **B**)

LARGE LEAF REPEAT (STENCIL **A**)

REVERSED FRUITS FRIEZE (STENCIL **B**)

LEAVES AND FRUIT PATTERN (STENCILS **B** AND **C**)

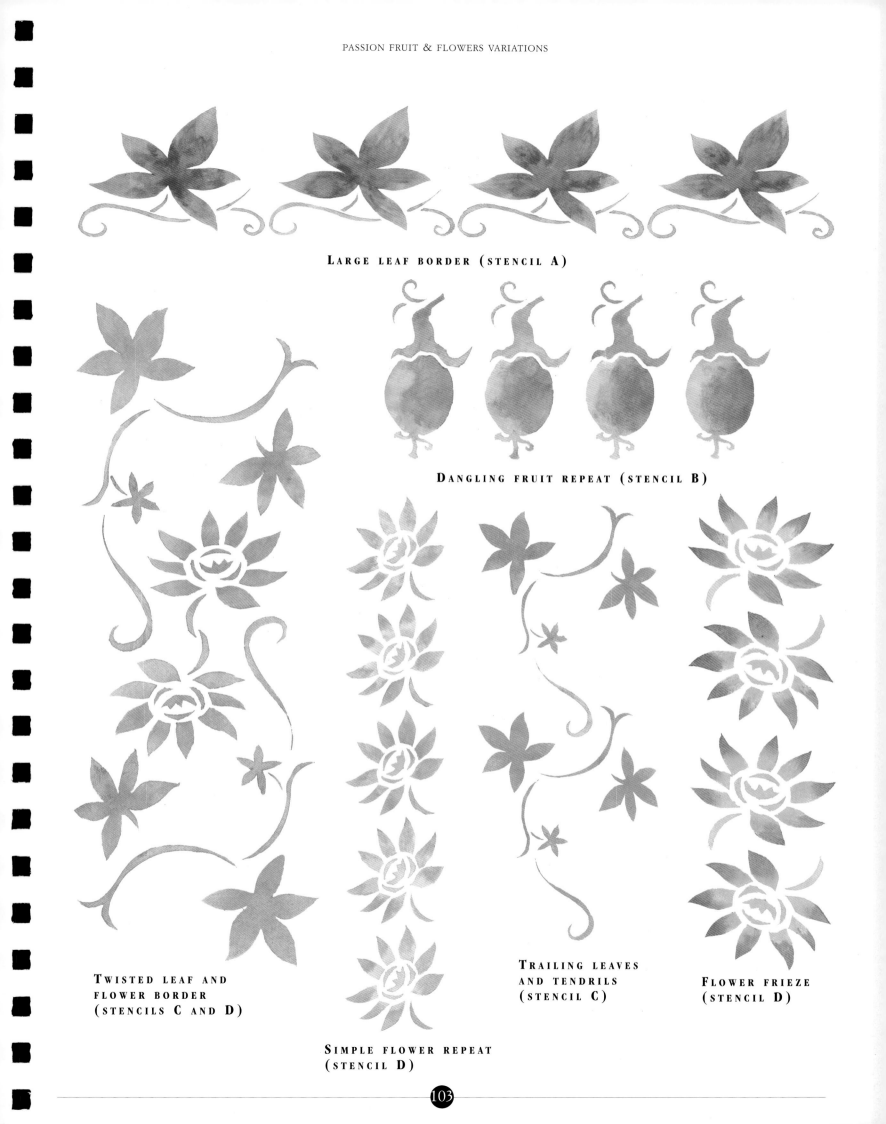

LARGE LEAF BORDER (STENCIL A)

DANGLING FRUIT REPEAT (STENCIL B)

TWISTED LEAF AND
FLOWER BORDER
(STENCILS C AND D)

TRAILING LEAVES
AND TENDRILS
(STENCIL C)

FLOWER FRIEZE
(STENCIL D)

SIMPLE FLOWER REPEAT
(STENCIL D)

# PEAS & BEANS

Trailing, tangled pea and bean leaves and pods are combined here to create an orderly yet delicate border design. The motifs give a country feel of newly picked produce, but the colors take the project into the area of modern interior design. Cool, fresh turquoise with green and cream, highlighted with stark white, creates a clean, crisp effect in contrast to the distressed, washed effect of the chair rail and tongue-and-groove boarding below.

## PAINT COLOR GUIDE

| | |
|---|---|
| Turquoise | Bright green |
| Cream | White |

### CREATING A BORDER FRIEZE

**1** Paint the wall you wish to stencil with turquoise latex paint.

**2** Carefully plan the design and measure the position of the stencils using tracing paper before painting them. Use green and cream paint for the running border of leaves (stencils A, C, D, G, and H), with the pod (stencil B) repeated in pairs in green. When dry, paint cream peas and beans in the pods (stencils E and F).

**3** Paint the chair rail in white first, then apply a cream wash on top.

**4** Paint the tongue-and-groove boarding in the same way, but use a turquoise base color with a cream wash on top.

### PROJECT PATTERN

This arrangement forms the basis of one repeat pattern on the wall in the photograph opposite. The peas and beans are stenciled on top of the pods.

H

C

D

G

A

B

B&E

### PLANNING THE DESIGN
Position the stencils in your desired pattern and draw the outlines on tracing paper. You can use this tracing to position your stencils all the way through the repeat. Simply attach the tracing to the wall with masking tape, then lift it up and down to slot in the appropriate stencil card.

### MATCHING THE REPEAT
To achieve an exact repeat every time, when you have finished the first pattern, move the tracing along the wall to where you want the design to be. With a permanent pen, trace the position of the first painted stencil so that all subsequent repeats will be equidistant.

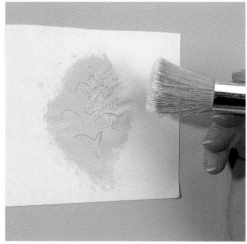

### HIGHLIGHTING THE MOTIFS
To enliven the design, apply white to the tops and edges of the leaves to highlight them. This gives the frieze a more delicate look and adds more dimension to the leaf shapes.

# PEAS & BEANS VARIATIONS

The rambling nature of these stencil designs makes this project incredibly versatile. You can twist and twine the patterns around the corners of walls or floors. You can even make them appear to grow over furniture and up onto the wall behind. Choose a starting point and simply let the stencil designs flow as naturally as possible. Remember to stand back regularly to check that the stencils look balanced.

**VEGETABLE LEAVES BORDER (STENCILS A AND G)**

**REFLECTED TENDRIL EDGING (STENCIL H)**

**LEAVES AND TENDRILS BORDER (STENCILS C AND H)**

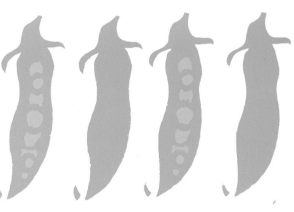

**PEA PODS FRIEZE (STENCILS B AND E)**

**LEFT: BEANS IN A ROW (STENCIL F)**

**BEAN PODS BORDER (STENCILS B AND F)**

**ABOVE: LINKING LEAVES REPEAT (STENCIL C)**

**PEA PODS AND
LEAVES FRIEZE
(STENCILS A AND B)**

**LEAF CIRCLE (STENCILS A, C, G, AND H)**

**FLOWERS AND PEAS IN ROWS
(STENCILS D AND E)**

# CHINESE POMEGRANATES

The familiar Chinese willow pattern inspired this design of pomegranates with flowers and leaves, and its cool blue-and-white color scheme is particularly suitable for a bathroom. The motifs can be used throughout the room—on the walls, the laundry basket, the bathtub, and even the windows. They make a dramatic-looking design when positioned closely together to create a border. Individual elements could also be used to simulate hand-blocked wallpaper using a symmetrical pattern.

## PAINT COLOR GUIDE

Bright blue

### DECORATING THE BATHTUB

**1** Paint the sides of the bathtub with a couple of coats of white paint.

**2** Position the solid pomegranate (stencil E) first, then put in a leaf and flower, making sure they do not touch. Then position the more delicate fruit (stencil C) at an angle. Follow this with a couple of flowers and a leaf.

**3** Trace the pattern to make the repeating process simpler. Slide the stencils under the tracing to the correct position, then remove the tracing to paint the stencil. Draw the position of the previous repeat onto the tracing paper to align the repeats correctly.

### PROJECT PATTERN

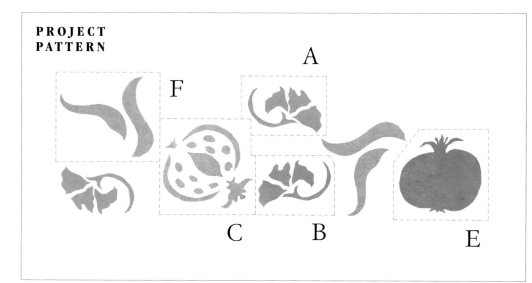

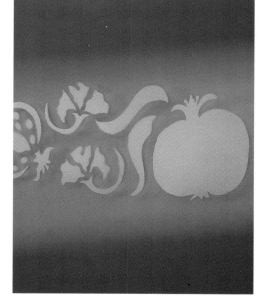

### SQUARING UP
Rather than spending hours putting plumb lines on the bathtub, use masking tape to stick a small level on the side of the tub. Then you can align and square up your stencil with the level. This makes repositioning much easier.

### REVERSING THE COLOR SCHEME
If you are working with a two-color scheme, it is fun to paint the combination the opposite way around somewhere else in the room. Dramatically contrasting colors work well, but use the technique with similar tones for a more subtle look.

### STENCILING ON WINDOWS
A lovely finish to the scheme can be achieved, especially in bathrooms, if you take the design onto the windows. Mark off the area around the stencil with newspaper and gently spray the stencil with clear or white spray—this gives a frosted or etched look.

# CHINESE POMEGRANATES VARIATIONS

Experiment in your bathroom with a different interpretation of the pomegranate design using aquatints of turquoise and cobalt, or ring the changes with a variation along the same theme. Choosing the right paint for the surface is always tricky. If you want to stencil an uneven surface such as wicker, use spray paint. Spray evenly, using thin coats, to keep the edges of the image well defined.

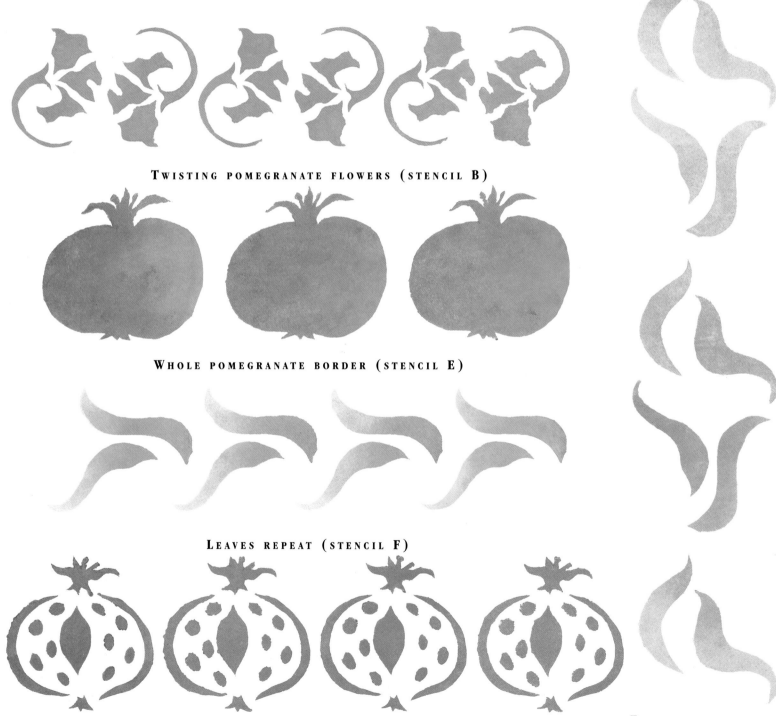

**TWISTING POMEGRANATE FLOWERS (STENCIL B)**

**WHOLE POMEGRANATE BORDER (STENCIL E)**

**LEAVES REPEAT (STENCIL F)**

**POMEGRANATE BORDER (STENCIL C)**

**FLOATING LEAVES (STENCILS D AND F)**

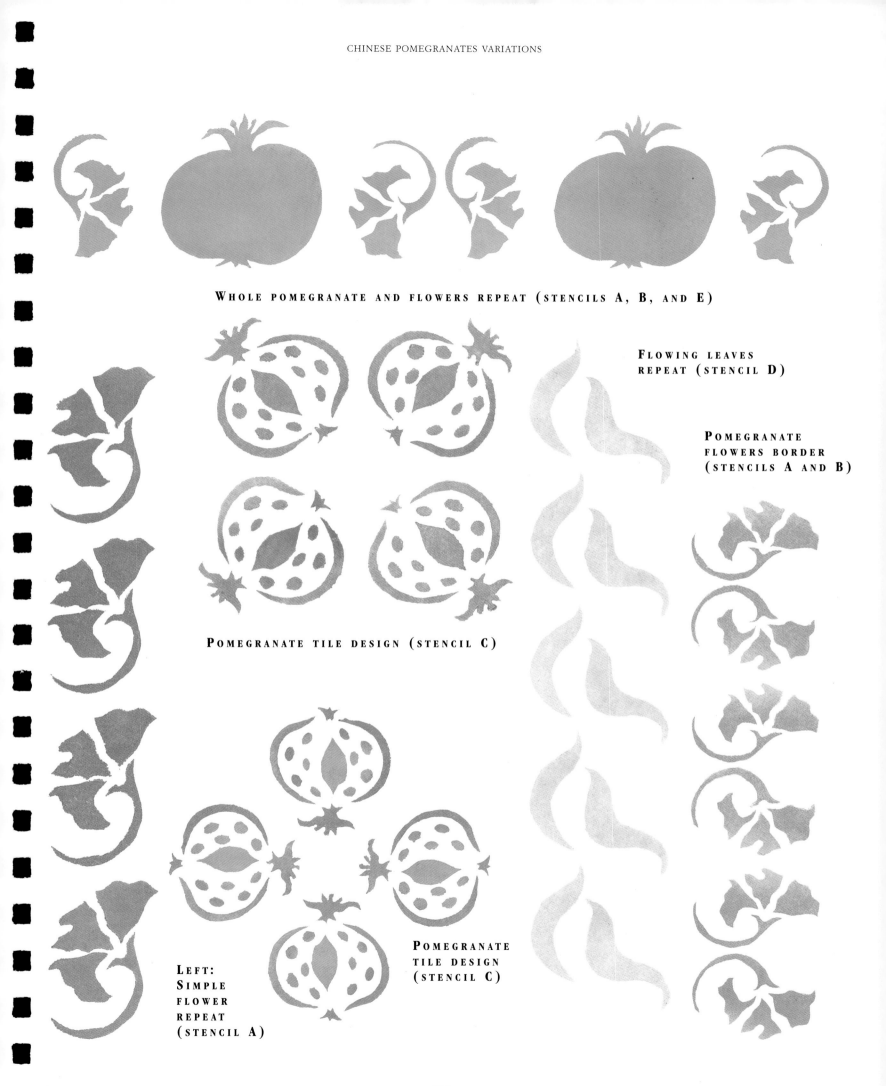

**WHOLE POMEGRANATE AND FLOWERS REPEAT (STENCILS A, B, AND E)**

**FLOWING LEAVES REPEAT (STENCIL D)**

**POMEGRANATE FLOWERS BORDER (STENCILS A AND B)**

**POMEGRANATE TILE DESIGN (STENCIL C)**

**POMEGRANATE TILE DESIGN (STENCIL C)**

**LEFT: SIMPLE FLOWER REPEAT (STENCIL A)**

# SUPPLIERS

Latex paints are easily obtainable from home stores and good hardware stores; contact manufacturers below for your nearest supplier. Oil sticks and acrylic paints can be obtained from art supply stores. Other stenciling supplies can usually be found in any of the above, and there are many dedicated stencil stores.

Stencil Artisans League Inc.
526 King Street, Ste. 423
Alexandria, VA 22314
(703) 518-4375
www.sali.org

Blue Ribbon Stencils
26 S. Horton Street
Dayton, OH 45403
(937) 254-2319
www.blueribbonstencils.com

The Mad Stencilist
P.O. Box 5497 Dept N
El Dorado Hills CA 95762
Toll free: (888) 88-B-Mad-2
www.madstencilist.com

Stenciling.com
Online Decorative Arts Community
Features a listing of tens of
online stencil suppliers.
www.stenciling.com

Published by Murdoch Books UK Ltd
First published in 2001, reprinted 2001

ISBN 1 85391 938 1
A catalogue record of this book is available from the British Library.
Copyright © Text, photography and design Murdoch Books UK Ltd 2001

Senior Project Editor: Anna Osborn
Design and Editorial Assistance: Axis Design
Photographer: Graeme Ainscough
Stylist: Caroline Davis and Clare Louise Hunt

CEO: Robert Oerton
Publisher: Catie Ziller
Production Manager: Lucy Byrne

Printed and bound in China through The Hanway Press Ltd

Murdoch Books UK Ltd
Ferry House, 51–57 Lacy Road,
Putney, London SW15 1PR
United Kingdom
Tel: +44 (0)20 8355 1480, Fax: +44 (0)20 8355 1499
Murdoch Books (UK) Ltd is a subsidiary of Murdoch Magazines Pty Ltd.

Murdoch Books ®
Pier 8/9 23 Hickson Road
Millers Point NSW 2000
Australia
Tel: +61 (0)2 8220 2000, Fax: +66 (0)2 8220 2020
Murdoch Books ® is a trademark of Murdoch Magazines Pty Ltd.

# DANDELIONS

A    B    C

D    E

F

G    H

I

J

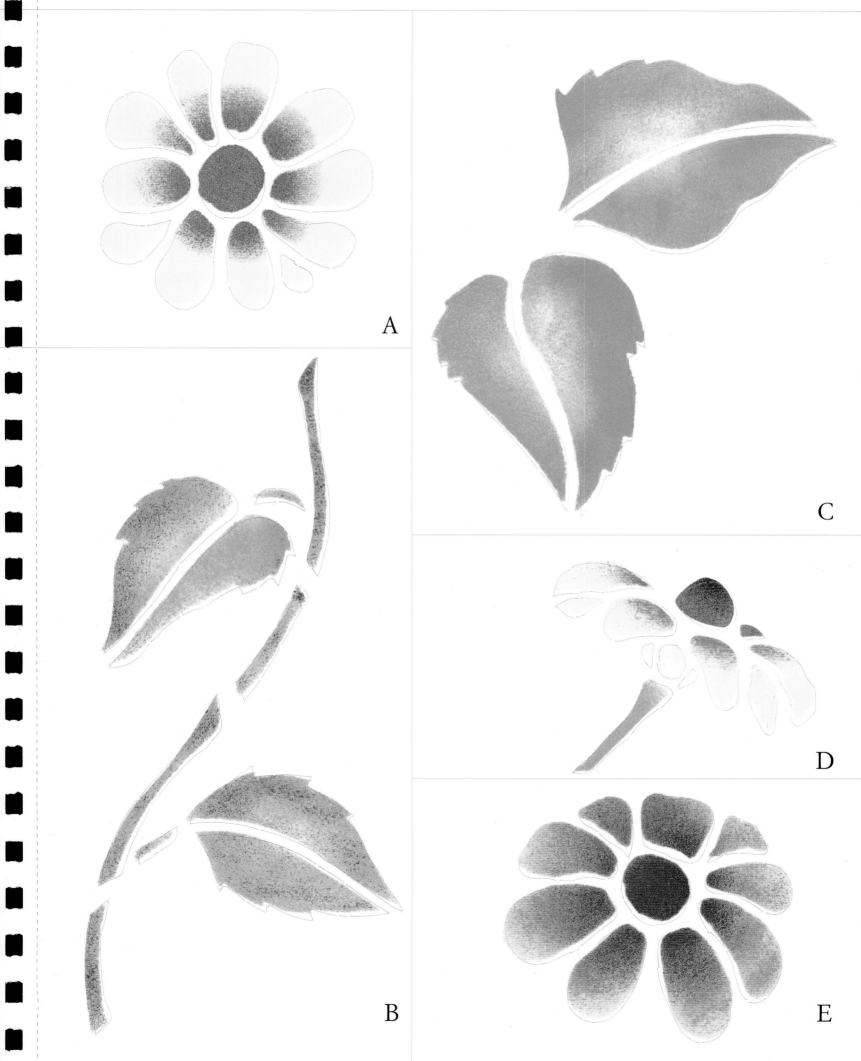

A

B

C

D

E

A

B

C

D

E

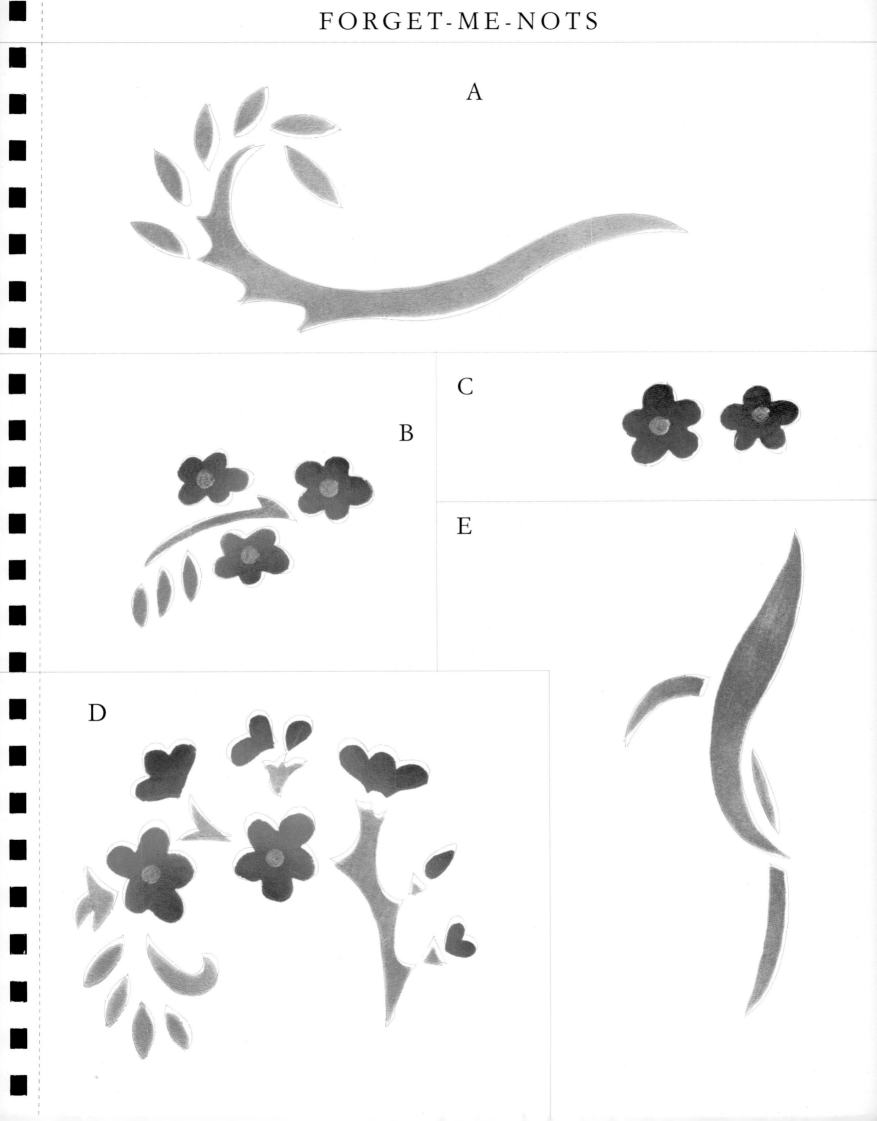

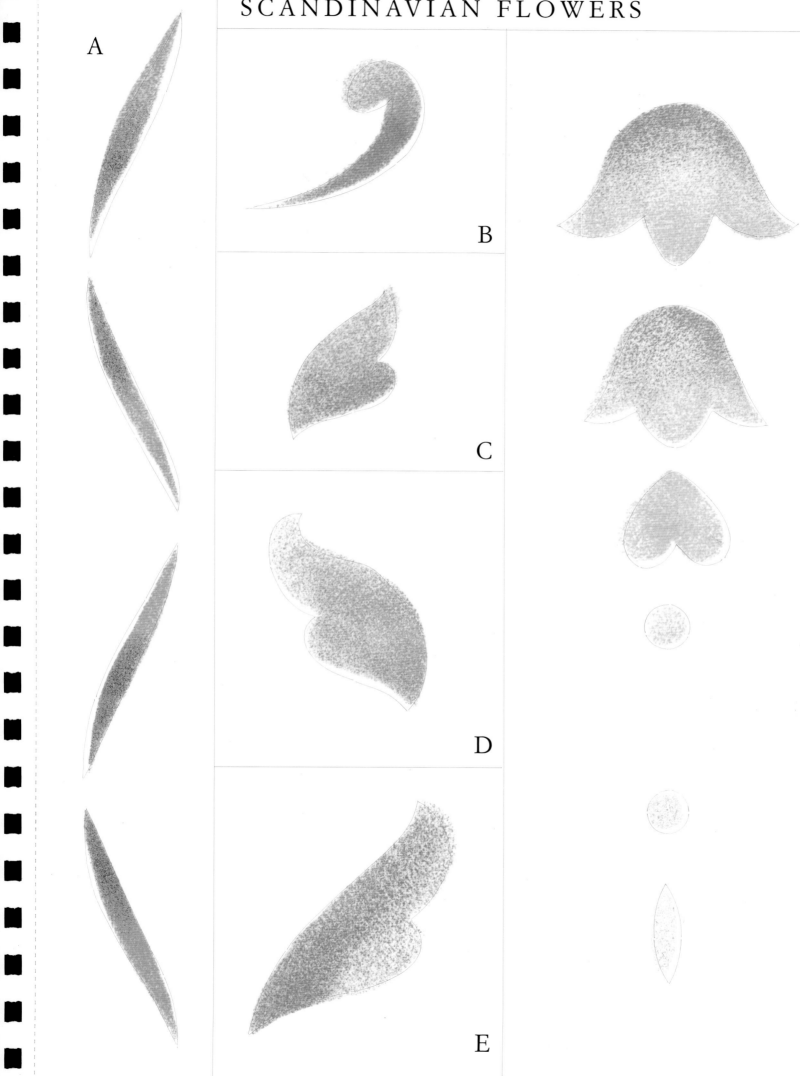

A

B

C

D

E

F

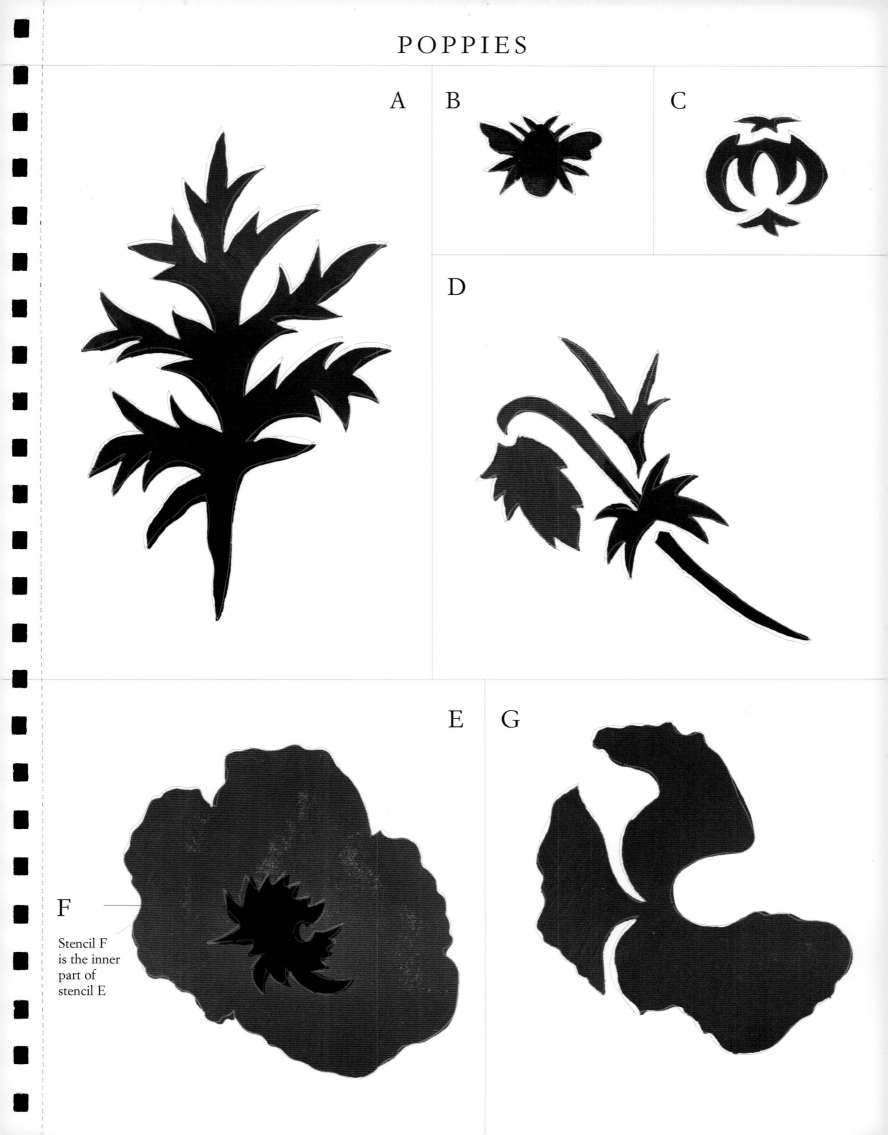

A

B

C

D

E  G

F

Stencil F
is the inner
part of
stencil E

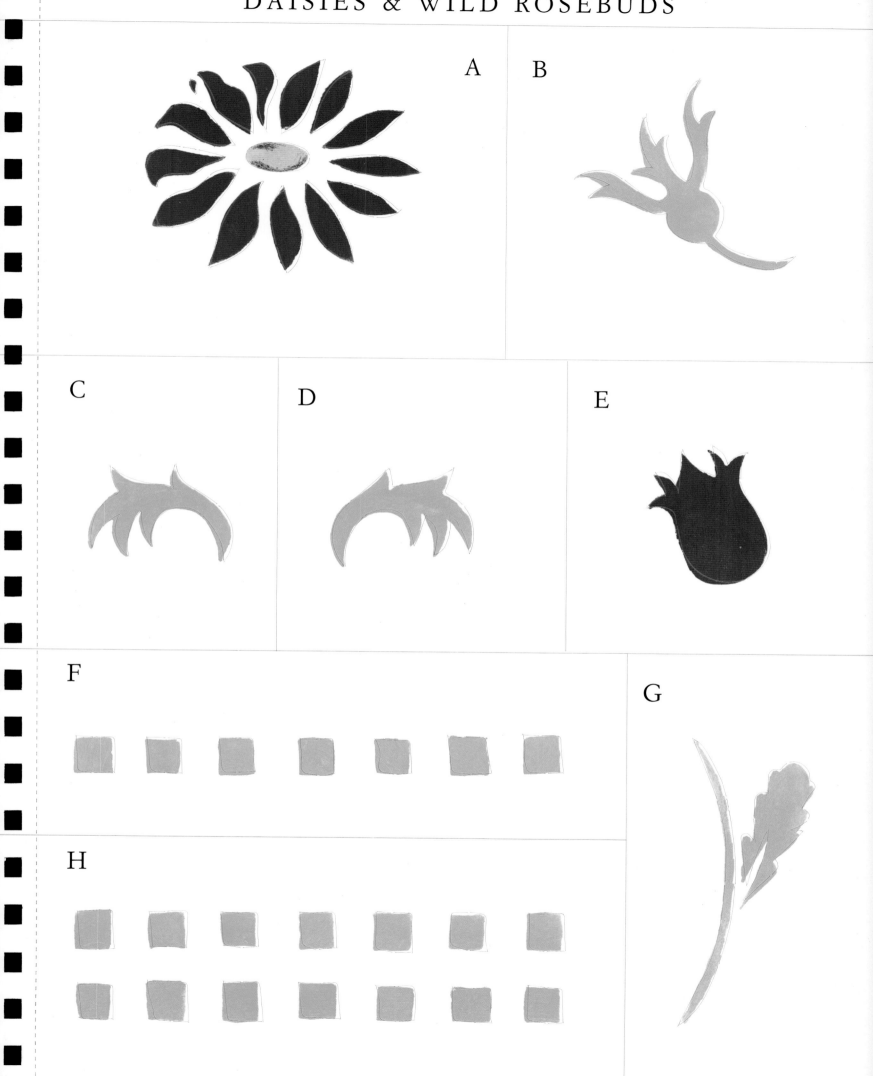

A

B

C

D

E

F

G

H

# CORNFLOWERS & BUTTERFLIES

A

B

C

D

E

F

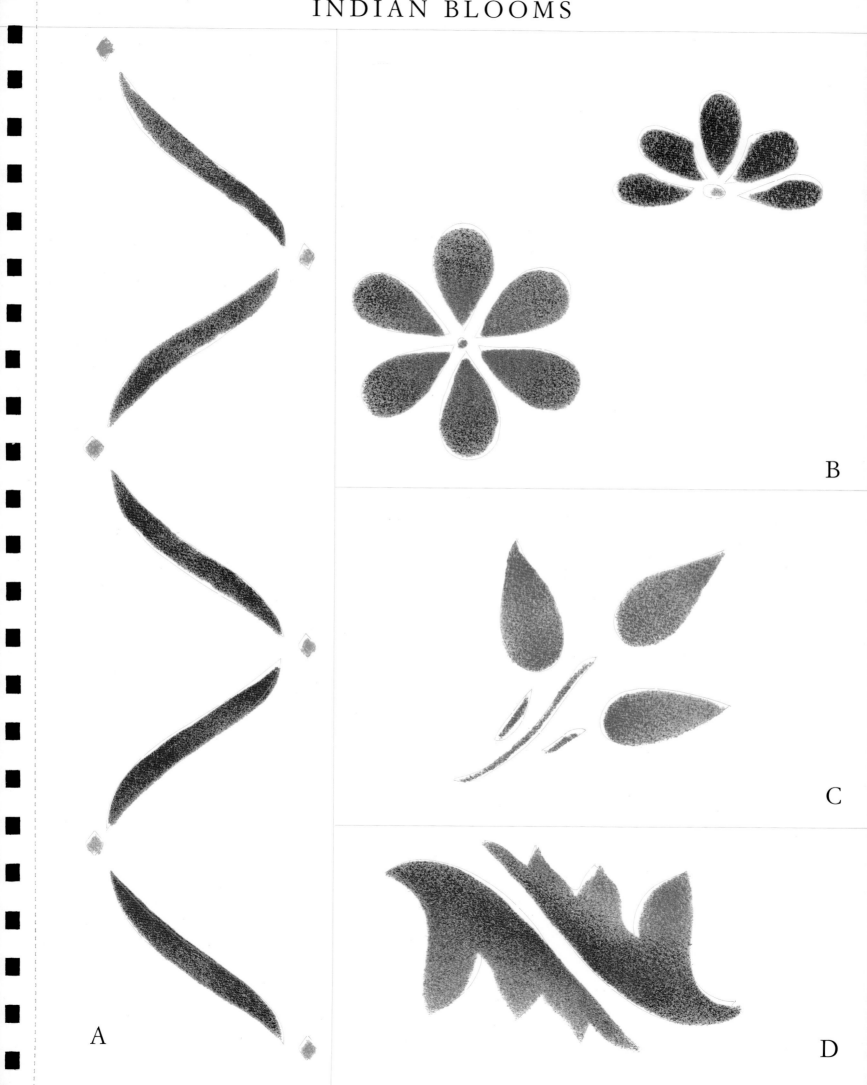

A

B

C

D

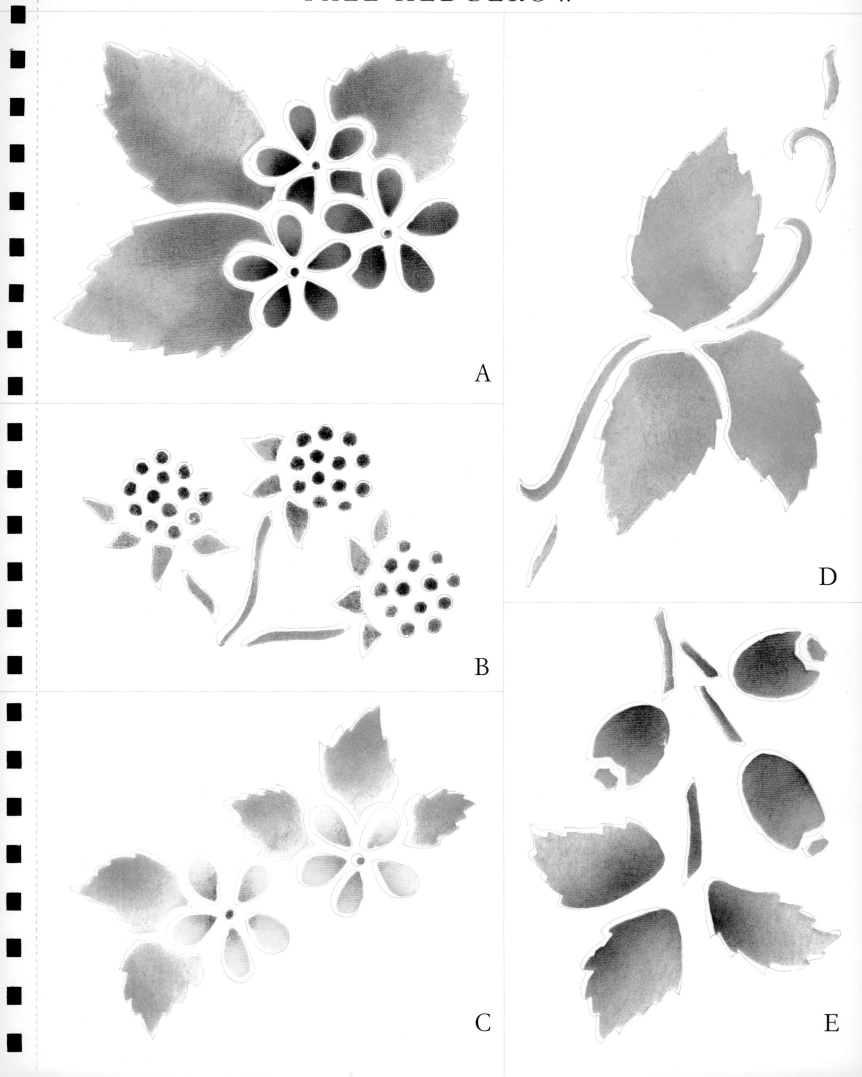

A

B

C

D

E

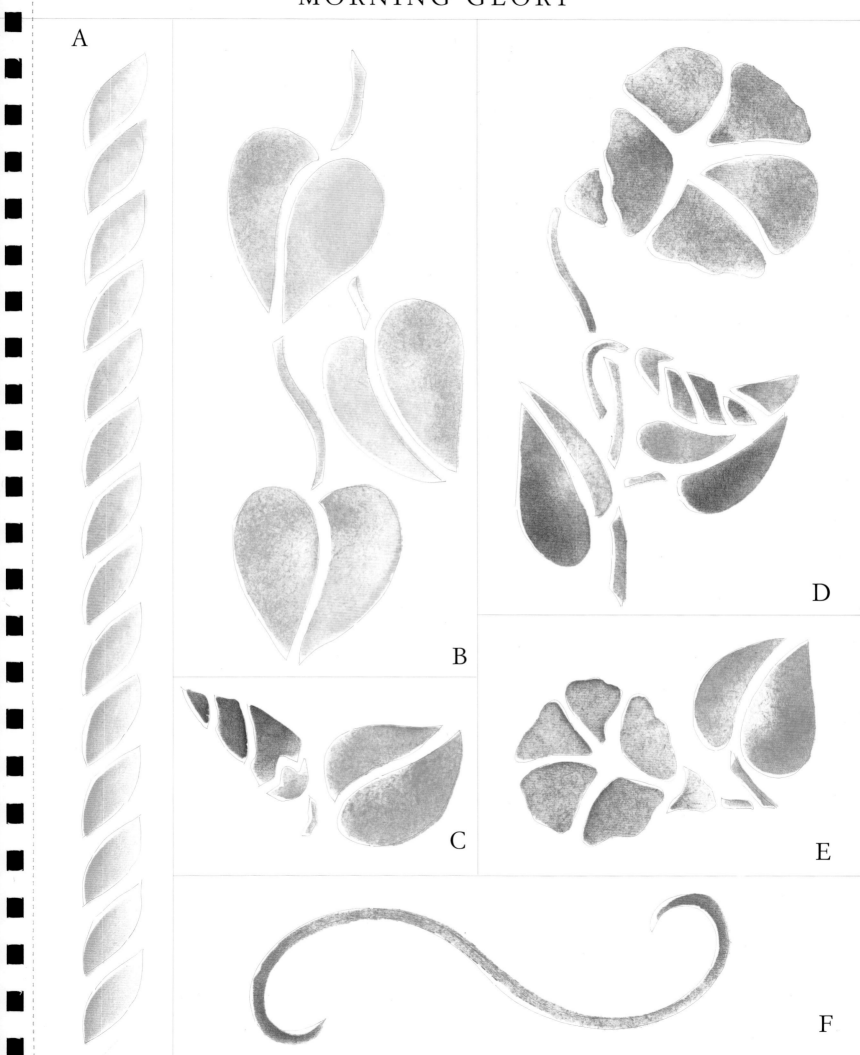

A

B

C

D

E

F

A

B

C

D

E

F

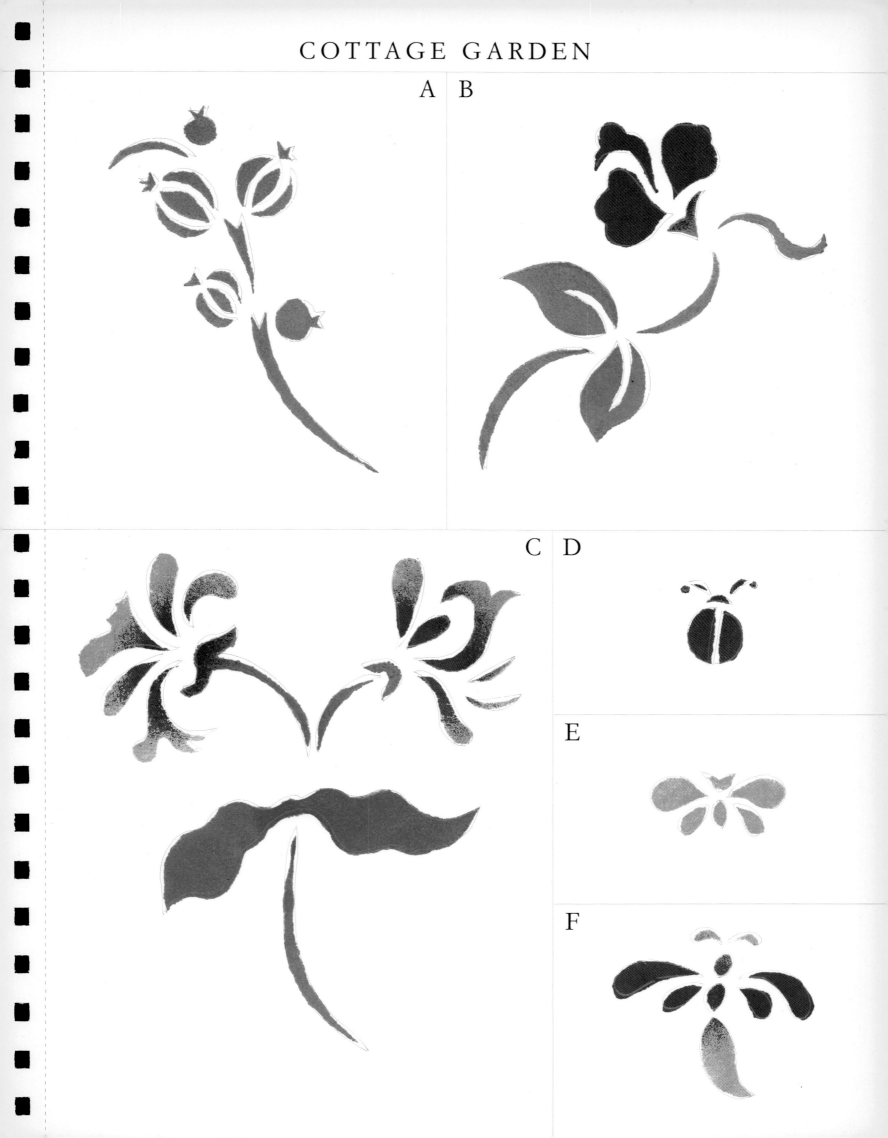

A B

C D

E

F

# PAISLEY HARVEST

A  B

C

D  E  F

A

B

C

D

E

F

G

H

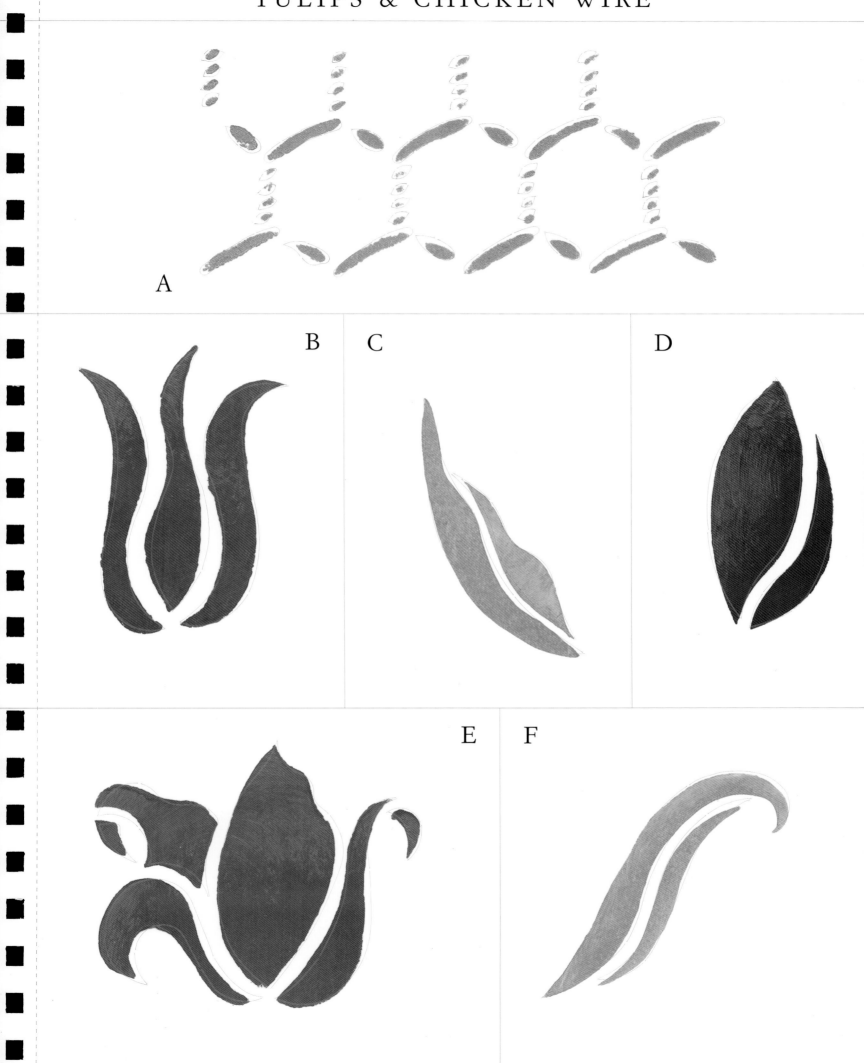

A

B

C

D

E

F

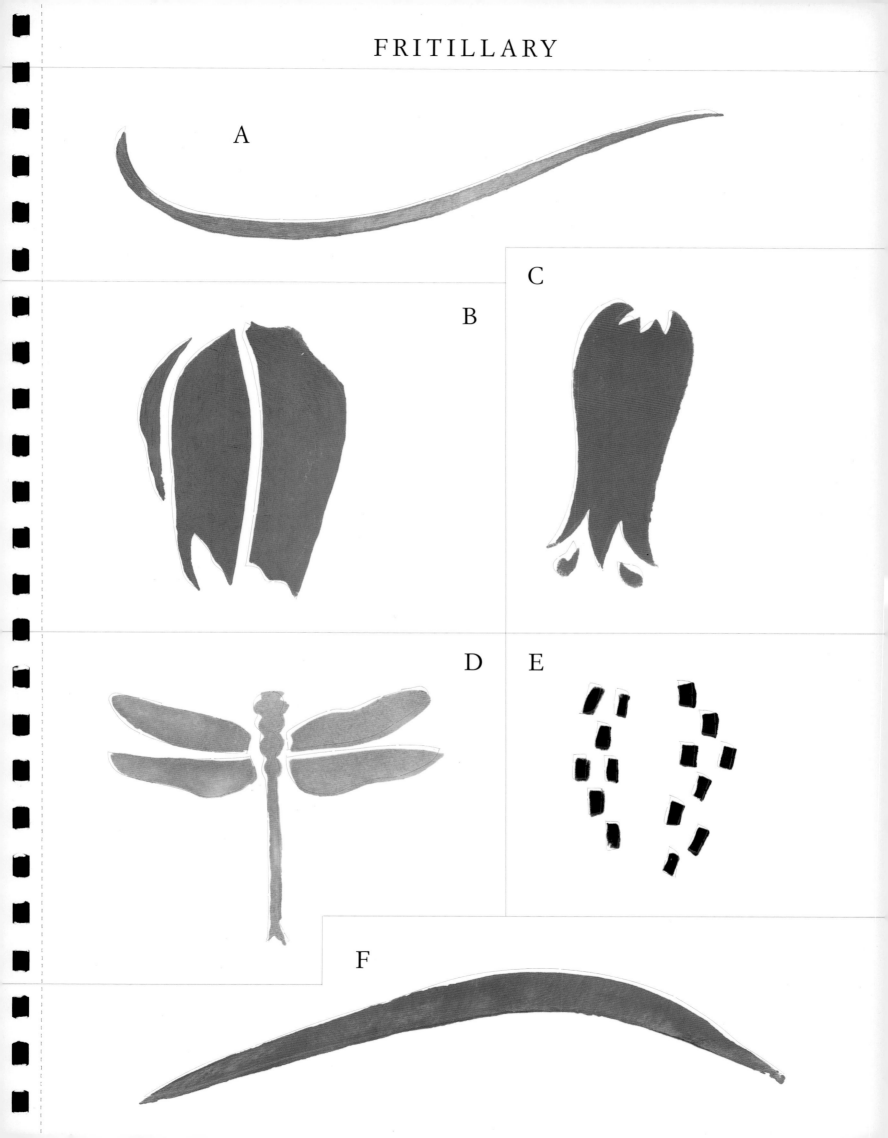

A

B

C

D

E

F

A

C

B

D

E

A B

C D

E F G

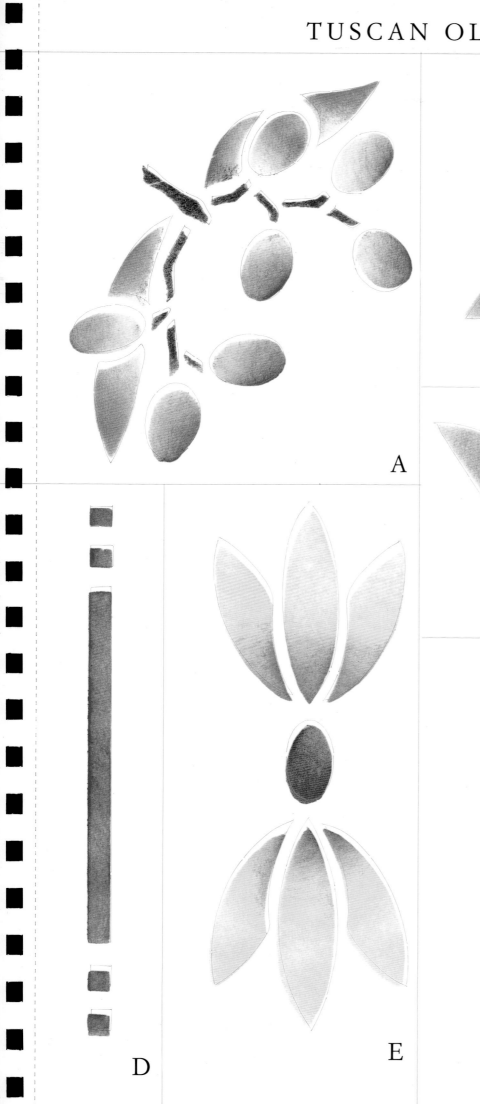

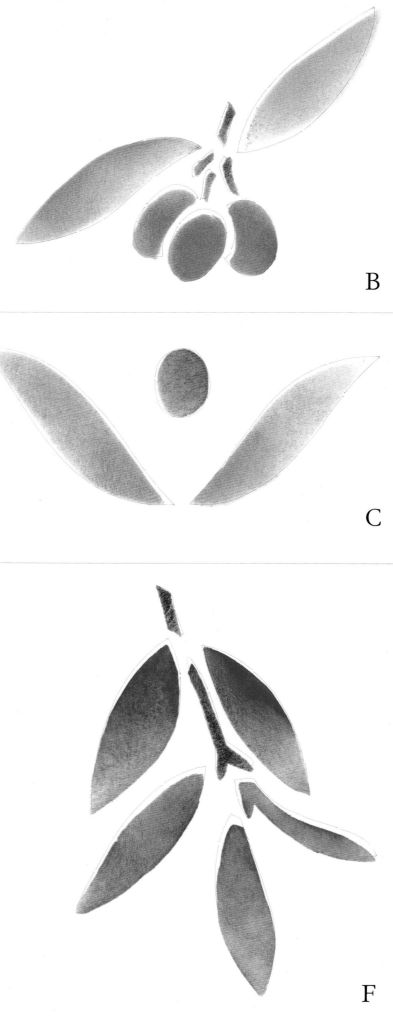

A

B

C

D

E

F

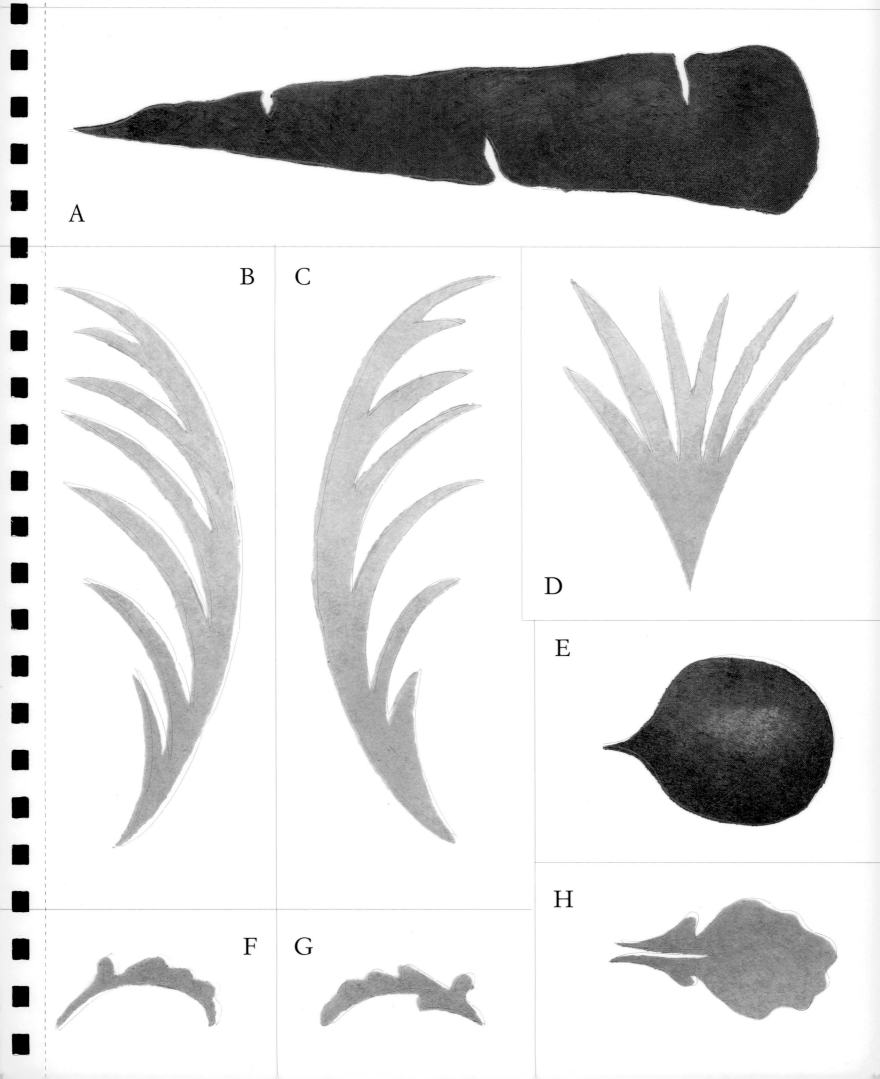

A

B  C

D

E

F  G  H

A

B

C

D

A

B

C

D

E

F

G

H

# CHINESE POMEGRANATES

A B

C D

E F

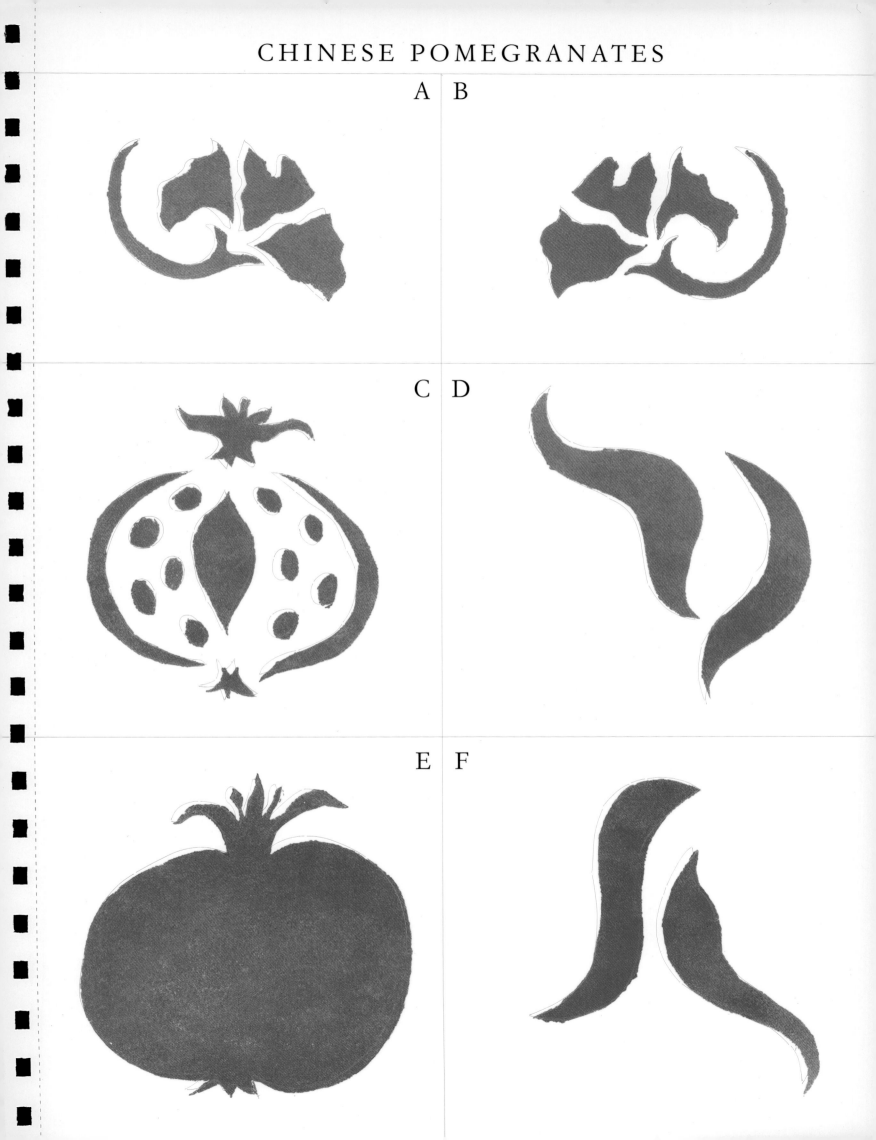